OUTSID

#INSIDETHEBOOK

AMG
PUBLISHERS

SANDIE
WILLIAMS

OUTSIDE THE BOX
#INSIDETHEBOOK
Copyright © 2024 by Sandie Williams
Published by AMG Publishers, Inc.

Print Edition ISBN 13: 978-1-61715-606-9

Editing and interior design by Rick Steele Editorial Services
(https://steeleeditorialservices.myportfolio.com)

Printed in the United States of America

Dedicated to your inner child
because to such belongs the kingdom of God

ACKNOWLEDGMENTS

I do not suffer from FOMO (Fear Of Missing Out); I suffer from FOLSO (Fear Of Leaving Someone Out) but here goes:

To all the children, named and unnamed, whose candid weekly wisdom helped me bring to life so many spiritual nuggets buried in The Book.

To the congregations who observed, especially those adults who let their own inner child play *outside the box* with us, and who encouraged me to "write this stuff down!"

To award-winning author Ann Marie Stewart, for edging me toward publication and for sharing her strong Christian principles and creative gifts with my family and others.

To my grammarian and prayer warrior, Lorrayne Haynes, who uses her chronic insomnia to create encouraging internet 'pun-gardens' to start my days with shalom.

To my many fond memories of Susan Ann Rau, especially those of our Alaskan Cruise adventures that sparked five chapters of spiritual nuggets in this volume.

To my parents, Jerry and Christine Toler, who named me Sandra, meaning 'helper of mankind', and then encouraged me to live up to it by being incredible role models.

To my BIRTH FAMILY and FAITH FAMILY far and wide: I pray that they ALL see their influence in the annals of my escapades in this volume.

To my life mate Bill, who leads me, carries me, pushes me, and occasionally drags me exhausted behind him as we accept each Mission Impossible our journey together challenges us to pursue. Thanks Hon, for the spiritual nuggets each pursuit yields!

To the distinguished and beloved Order of the Brats, daughters Wendie and BrieDanielle, son Chalon and his wife Simone who, together with the steady parade of Brat-status friends they bring under our roof, leverage constant fresh inspiration.

To granddaughter Rowan and grandsons Tristan and Leif, the 2.0 version of their parents. Interaction with this new generation, filtered through their 21st Century mindsets and upsets, attests to the timelessness of the great I AM.

To the great I AM—Creator, Savior and Counselor who has never been nor will be the great I WAS. I still see glimpses of God everywhere and in everything; although it now seems to be at the speed of Light! I just pray that I can keep up:

And even when I am old and gray, O God, do not forsake me, until I declare Your strength to this generation, Your power to all who are to come. (Psalm 71:18) Amen.

INTRODUCTION

You hold in your hand a volume of unADULTerated wisdom gained from interacting with "the least of these." It is a quirky collection of true episodes that recount my adventures as God's weekly messenger to children for over 40 years. Now, in printed form, it speaks to the child in all of us.

Years ago, a New Age coworker informed me the office machines were on the fritz because Mercury was in retrograde. When I objected to her comment, she told me I should learn to think outside the box. I ended the confrontation by telling her I had no problem thinking outside the box as long as it stayed inside "The Book." That incident stuck with me and later inspired the title of my manuscript.

In 2014 *Merriam-Webster* added "hashtag" to its dictionary, defining it as "You know a thing is *really a thing* these days when it has its own hashtag." Thus, #InsideTheBOOK is meant to convey to this generation of readers that **the Bible is *really a thing!***

Outside the Box #InsideTheBOOK contains a year of devotional vignettes to jumpstart each busy week in the Word. I often used outlandish shenanigans that were well outside the "church" box to illustrate timeless spiritual truths for all ages. Together, the children and I would bring them to life, all the while sowing scriptural seeds that would continue to grow in their hearts and bear fruit in their lives.

I would routinely get some very curious looks from salesclerks as I shopped for props while my mind was busy prepping my message. Ephesians 5:16 (NIV) encourages us to "make the most of every opportunity" so I would often share my evangelistic intentions for the items in my cart at the register. The shoppers in line behind me would be grinning and commenting, and one salesclerk even sent me on my way with, "Boy, I wish I didn't have to work. I'd love to visit your church just to see this!"

My own children did a lot of eye-rolling in front of their church friends but confessed that they were secretly laughing at my antics inside. Adults, on the other hand, would say, "You crack me up!" "Was that rehearsed?" "I hope you are writing this stuff down."

So, I did.

However, I want this book to do more than just share what biblical relevance has been gleaned from both mundane and bizarre incidents in my own life. In lighthearted and tear-jerking ways, it is meant to encourage young and old alike to find their own glimpses of God everywhere and in everything.

Today, we live in a culture that is almost a blank canvas. If we do not share those divine insights in a world gone sideways, who will?

SANDIE WILLIAMS

From childhood you have known the sacred writings which are able to give you the wisdom that leads to salvation through faith which is in Christ Jesus. All Scripture is inspired by God and beneficial for teaching, for rebuke, for correction, for training in righteousness; so that the man or woman of God may be fully capable, equipped for every good work. (2 Timothy 3:15-17)

But God has chosen the foolish things of the world to shame the wise, and God has chosen the weak things of the world to shame the things which are strong. (1 Corinthians 1:27)

From the mouths of infants and nursing babies You have established strength because of Your enemies, to do away with the enemy and the revengeful. (Psalm 8:2)

CONTENTS xi

Chapter ONE
SCISSORS AND KNIVES

"**I** just finished wallpapering my living room at home," I announced as the kids took their places around me. I didn't know how hard it was going to be, but it was a big job! The directions made it sound so simple.

"*First you find your starting point and then you have to* **plumb** *it.*" I reached into my bag for my visual aid. "I always thought plumbing was hooking up water pipes, but it also means using gravity to mark a true vertical line." I showed them the string with a weight hanging from it.

"*Then after you measure how long your first piece needs to be, you have to cut it.*" I removed a pair of wallpapering scissors from my bag. From handles to point, they were easily 20" long. "I could not have done the job without these mega-scissors," I declared, brandishing them menacingly. "They were fantastic. Sharp too! Would you like to see how well they work?"

"Yeah!" they shouted.

"All right then." I motioned my husband to come forward as I confided to the kids, "I noticed this morning that his nose hairs need cutting."

With that, he stopped in his tracks.

"No thanks!" he said, emphatically. "You're not going to use those on me!"

"Why not? I already told you they worked great cutting the wall-paper."

"That may be true, but they won't work for cutting nose hairs."

I looked at the kids. "What's his problem?"

One budding young scientist in the group said, "They're too big. It could hurt him."

I looked at my husband.

"Is that what you're afraid of?" I asked him.

"Yes, and you're not coming near me with those things. I'll use my own scissors, thank you very much."

With that, he dug his junior Swiss tool out of his pocket and showed us the tiny scissors. The cutting edge was about a half an inch long. "These are what I use, and they are just perfect!"

The kids nodded in agreement. I stuck my hand out. He started to give me his scissors but, instead, I took his hand in mine. I grabbed his fingers and did a quick inspection.

"Aha! Just as I suspected."

"What?" he demanded.

"You didn't get the grime out from under your fingernails after you changed the oil in your car yesterday. Wait right here. The kids and I can fix that."

I reached into my bag and pulled out a butcher knife that was almost too long for my kitchen drawer.

"Ack! Don't even think about it!" he warned as his hand disappeared behind his back.

"Come on, it will just take a second. We promise. I washed it really well after I boned the chicken last night."

You are *not* going to use it on *this* chicken," he said pointing to himself.

"Chicken, chicken!" The kids took up the taunt,

"Oh yeah? Watch this! He held up his junior Swiss tool and extracted the tiny knife blade. With a quick swipe under the offending nail, he removed a black sliver. "There! Job done, so you can put away that lethal weapon."

With that, he turned on his heel and stalked off before we could think of something else to subject him to.

I looked at the kids. "Well, how about that! Apparently, BIG is not always BETTER. In fact, in some cases, BIG may not even work at all." My voice got nearly as big as the kids' eyes.

"So next time some big person tells you that you are too little to help do God's work, remind them that Jesus said that everyone should '*become as little children.*'

"And when the heavenly jobs are passed out in God's kingdom, The Book says a 'little child shall lead them.'"

Truly I say to you, unless you change and become like children, you will not enter the kingdom of heaven. (Matthew 18:3)

And the wolf will dwell with the lamb, and the leopard will lie down with the young goat, and the calf and the young lion and the fattened steer will be together; and a little boy will lead them. (Isaiah 11:6)

AUTHOR SANDIE WILLIAMS DOING HER BEST IMPERSONATION OF KEVIN SPLASHING AFTERSHAVE IN HOME ALONE

Chapter TWO

HOME ALONE

"I love the movie *Home Alone*," I said, holding up the DVD. "From the first implausible event of having, accidentally, left one of your children behind while leaving on a holiday vacation, to the eventual family reunion, the film entertains.

"The exploits of the young son, Kevin, as he thwarts would-be thieves time and time again are resourceful and effective. They range from simple deterrents to their gaining entry to methods designed to inflict real pain and do significant damage.

"But do the thieves give up?" My kids, caught up in their own memories of the movie, all shook their heads, emphatically.

"No. They keep coming back with renewed determination, and they keep leaving, angry and frustrated.

"Kevin almost seems to be enjoying the game. He understands that his adversaries will not give up easily, and he wastes no time after each onslaught preparing for the next invasion. In fact, he lays traps on multiple points of entry so he will be prepared for whatever route they take.

"When Jesus spent forty days in the wilderness preparing for His ministry, Satan visited Him, repeatedly. Each encounter was confrontational, with high stakes and fiendish promises.

"Jesus countered each one with real truth, defeating His opponent time and time again. But Satan *never gave up*, even when Jesus had finally let His adversary know that He was not going to fall for any of his offers.

"Jesus told Satan to go away (Matthew 4:10), and he did, but Luke's version of Christ's temptation tells us the devil was going to be watching for a chance to try again. It says, '...he left Him, *until an opportune time.*' (Luke 4:13)

"If The Book makes it clear that the devil was never going to stop tempting Jesus, it is a foregone conclusion that he will also never stop tempting each of us.

"But The Book also says, 'Resist the devil, and he will flee from you.' (James 4:7). He will be angry and frustrated, but he will leave—for the moment.

"And in that moment, use the time to regroup. Shore up weakened defenses and shaken spiritual confidence. Plan actual maneuvers designed to inflict actual damage on Satan and his unholy angels.

"The Ten Commandments is not just a list of dos & don'ts hanging on the wall at church that you get a Sunday School prize for memorizing. Each of them is like a door, a window; simply put, a point of entry that could be used by Satan. As was made so clear in *Home Alone*, laying traps that will guard you from his attacks at each of those points is child's play! You never know which one he will use, and he is very sneaky about it.

I pointed to the cover of the DVD and imitated Kevin's famous movie expression; eyes wide, hands-on cheeks and my mouth open in alarm. *"Could it be,"* I asked the kids, *"that he was about to utter that simple phrase that we all hear thrown about so casually?* It may seem harmless but flippantly exclaiming, *Oh My God!*, or even *OMG*, is actually breaking the third commandment, 'Do not take the Lord's name in vain' (Exodus 20:7, paraphased). Not saying it slams that door in Satan's face with an emphatic 'not falling for it, but nice try.'

"Remember when Kevin got banished to the attic? He asked his mother why everybody hated him. The Book tells us that hating someone is the same as murdering them in your heart. The fifth commandment says, 'You shall not murder' (Exodus 20:13).

"OK," I prompted my flock, "does everyone in Kevin's family seem to have a case of the grumpies?" No one disagreed so I added, "Ah, but you see, Satan was taking advantage of that open door and the commandment about hating and murdering was being broken by the whole family."

I had the distinct hunch that I was starting to hit a little too close to home, not just describing entertaining cinema, so I shifted gears.

"Guess what? The sixth commandment has a special perk that often gets overlooked because we don't always quote the whole thing: " 'Honor your father and mother,' . . . 'THAT IT MAY TURN OUT WELL FOR YOU. . . . ' " (Ephesians 6:3, [emphasis added]).

"Remember when Kevin angrily told his mother he wished his family would disappear? When he finds himself home alone, he is temporarily excited that he got his wish but, after a bit, begins to miss his family.

"When the thieves begin their attempts to break into the family home, he does a very good job of keeping that commandment. Instead of hating his parents for leaving him behind, he honors them by doing his best to keep their home safe and secure. And, sure enough, it goes **very well for him!**

"Just as was evident in *Home Alone*," I began, pointing at each of my listeners slowly and individually, "YOU and YOU and YOU can regard the temptations of life as a contest that YOU are going to enjoy winning.

"Our little hero never once says to himself, 'I am too young and too small. I am outnumbered.' In fact, after a few successes, even his initial fears are overcome. He begins to shrewdly assess every object in the house as a potential weapon at his disposal.

"Finally, remember our power has a divine Source, and The Book assures us that we are never really alone . . . at home or anywhere."

And so when the devil had finished every temptation, he left Him until an opportune time. (Luke 4:13)

Submit therefore to God. But resist the devil, and he will flee from you. (James 4:7)

And you shall not swear falsely by My name, so as to profane the name of your God; I am the LORD. (Leviticus 19:12)

HONOR YOUR FATHER AND MOTHER *(which is the first commandment with a promise)* SO THAT IT MAY TURN OUT WELL FOR YOU, AND THAT YOU MAY LIVE LONG ON THE EARTH. (Ephesians 6:2-3)

Everyone who hates his brother or sister is a murderer, and you know that no murderer has eternal life remaining in him. (1 John 3:15)

Where can I go from Your Spirit? Or where can I flee from Your presence? If I go up to the heavens, You are there; if I make my bed in the depths, You are there. (Psalm 139: 7-8, NIV)

Chapter THREE

THE SON

Dressed in goth black, I strode purposefully to the front of the sanctuary. My black fingernail polish and lipstick, combat boots, chain around one bicep, spiked dog collar around my neck, a nose ring linked to one creepy earring, a tattoo, and electric blue hair swept into a mohawk got a unanimous reaction. Indignantly, I announced, "I went somewhere last night where I was not welcome!"

The children, who had begun their trek to our customary place at the front of the church, took one look at me and fled back to their parents. I glared at a few of the older ones who stood their ground, until they conceded the match and retreated.

After the shocked gasps and giggles had subsided, I asked my husband and two other couples to stand. They were, of course, attired in their Sunday-casual best dress.

"Last night," I went on, "we went to a place in the city called Studio Seven. We walked to the ticket counter dressed pretty much the way you see they are dressed this morning, with my elegant friend Linda, here, leading the way." A ripple of appreciative applause for their appropriate choice of attire erupted.

"For those of you who may not be aware, Studio Seven is a warehouse where heavy metal bands go to perform before crowds dressed as you see me here. Believe me," I informed them, shaking my head, "my get-up this morning is tame compared to that of last night's counterculture. The relentless barrage of noise coming from the stage was ear-splitting, vulgar, violent, distinctly dark, and disturbing."

"As we approached, the man at the door looked us up and down. Then he snarled, 'I think you folks are in the wrong place.' "

"No," said my undaunted companion, "we are here for the 9:30 show."

"Lady, do you know what we do in here?"

"No!" she admitted defiantly, but still stood her ground.

"Do you know what kind of music this is?" he asked, as if totally oblivious to the fact that, even outside the entrance, the amplified din emanating from the building was so loud it actually shook the sidewalk we were standing on."

Not to be dissuaded, she countered, "Yes, I think the whole *neighborhood* knows what kind of music it is, but we came to hear my son."

The man's transformation was instantaneous. "Oh," he nodded, "your *son* is in the band."

Without further argument, he collected our entrance fee, stamped our hands, and sent us into the smoky interior. We were immediately the object of considerable curiosity, amusement, resentment, and even a tiny ripple of contained hostility. In an upper loft, we found a good vantage point with our earplugs furtively inserted.

For my wide-eyed audience of children and the parents they were clinging to as if I were a scary movie character, I took my fingers out of my ears and asked them a question.

"Now, for those of you who have been hanging on my every word, what made the difference to our acceptance?"

"The son," the entire congregation whispered in a unison sigh.

"That is absolutely correct," I confirmed. "We were there to hear him perform his final concert and would have been disappointed if we had been denied that experience."

"You know, there was an extremely important moment recorded in The Book that set the stage for God's church on earth. It is what we call "The Transfiguration." There, the Law (Moses), the Prophets (Elijah), and the Gospel (Jesus) came together. This was so important that God, Himself, had to get their attention. A cloud enveloped them all, and there was no mistaking the Voice that commanded: "This is my Son whom I love. Listen to Him!" My voice bellowed throughout the church as if on a God-mic. I let the sound echo.

"God's church on earth has been providing a place ever since, where the words of the Son can be heard regularly and accurately." I let that sink in as parents hugging their children, nodded slowly.

Then to the childish faces that were still not sure what to make of me, but with the words directed to the hearts of their parents, I concluded.

"So, if a group of people show up at the door of our church some Sunday dressed as you see me now, they may LOOK as if they don't belong and, truth be known, their demeanor and their music are pretty accurate reflections of the dark and unhappy world they live in.

BUT

If they say they came to hear **the Son**, they are absolutely in the right place!

Then a cloud formed, overshadowing them, and a voice came out of the cloud:

"This is My beloved Son; listen to Him!" (Mark 9:7)

Chapter
FOUR
A BOX
OF
DARK

"**I** have brought something very interesting to show you this morning," I said, holding up a small box about six inches square, as the children came forward.

"There is a peephole at one end, so you can all take a look inside." One by one, they squinted into the hole until one of the braver ones finally said, disgustedly,

"I can't see anything. It's dark in there."

They all nodded and agreed, relieved that someone had finally spoken up.

"Well of course you can't see anything in there," I countered. "There isn't anything else in there but dark. It's a whole box of dark."

I held it aloft, proudly. The kids looked at me like I had lost my mind.

"I thought maybe we could take it out, pass it around, examine it a little." With that, I threw open the lid.

The youngest ones giggled at that absurd notion, and several of the older ones said,

"You can't do that."

They practically roared at the look on my face as I stared down at the open box.

"What? I was sure it was still in here. It must have leaked out through the peep hole." I turned the box over on its side, examining it closely.

Conner, the general spokesman for the group, rolled his eyes and sighed at my stupidity.

"I told you, you can't do that. Dark is only dark until the light hits it. Then it isn't dark anymore."

"Well, I'll be." I said, shaking my head as I slapped my thigh. "That must be what it means in The Book when it says that light is stronger than darkness.

"Isn't it interesting that if you open a small box of dark in a lighted room, it disappears, and if you light a candle in a dark room, the big dark disappears?" The kids quieted in consideration.

"According to The Book, *Jesus came to be the Light of the world.* He's certainly the *Son* of the one true God who has no darkness in Him, isn't He?"

The kids all nodded in agreement.

"But not the sun in the sky," Conner clarified.

"So, what is His kind of Light?"

"It's sort of how we know what to do instead of being bad," a brave little girl volunteered.

"Ahh!" I agreed. "When it's really dark, people sometimes get away with doing bad things because they think they are hidden. In fact," I paused and panned my audience, "When you want to try and get away with something you know is wrong, aren't you kind of sneaky about it?" Several of the kids nodded sheepishly. Their parents grinned.

"The more times you do things that you know are wrong, and get away with it, the easier it becomes. I think that is what The Book means when it says '*the darkness has blinded them.*' After a while, bad people don't even know they are being bad and that's really sad, isn't it?"

The kids nodded glumly.

"But there is a solution!" I raised my finger. "The Book also tells us to *'shine our own light in the darkness.'* Remember what happens when you light even a small candle when the power goes out?"

"There's no more dark."

"It's not so scary."

"I know where to walk."

"Wow," I interrupted. You just quoted something else The Book says. You probably didn't even know it, huh!" They shrugged collectively.

I held my hands out as I called my left hand *dark* and my right hand *light*. I weighed them up and down a few times; dark, light, dark, light.

Two choices! Which to choose? If you don't want to be 'left' in the dark, wandering around, all alone, don't choose the left one!" I dropped my left hand decisively to my side.

"If you want to know where to walk, choose the 'right' one. Jesus said, 'if you walk in the light as I am in the light, you be able to enjoy all the friends you can see are around you.' (I John 1:7, paraphrased). Not only that, your own light will shine, and those poor people who were 'left' in the dark may want to come out and join you!"

I raised my right hand as high as I could and started bringing my left hand up to join it as I spun slowly in a circle, smiling. "After awhile, the light starts to spread, and the world gets a whole lot brighter."

The light shines in the darkness, and the darkness doesn't extinguish the light. (John 1:5, CEV)

Then Jesus again spoke to them, saying, "I am the Light of the world; the one who follows Me will not walk in the darkness, but will have the Light of life." (John 8:12)

But the one who hates his brother or sister is in the darkness and walks in the darkness, and does not know where he is going because the darkness has blinded his eyes. (1 John 2:11)

God is light; and in him there is no darkness at all. (1 John 1:5b)

But if we walk in the Light as He Himself is in the Light, we have fellowship with one another, and the blood of Jesus His Son cleanses us from all sin. (1 John 1:7)

Your light must shine before people in such a way that they may see your good works, and glorify your Father who is in heaven. (Matthew 5:16)

Chapter
FIVE

COUNTING HAIRS

"We have a big huge job ahead of us today," I told the kids coming up the aisle of the sanctuary, "We need to get started quickly, so I am going to pick a couple of volunteers to help me." I chose the first two who made it to the altar steps—tow-headed brothers who were about ten and six years old.

I asked little Patrick if he could stand very still for a while. He nodded agreeably.

"OK," I turned to his older brother, Matthew, "What I need you to do is to count the hairs on his head." The congregation began to laugh softly but, obedient little guy that he was, he went right to work.

While he was busy with the task, I told the rest of the kids.

"While I was having my devotions this week, I came across something in The Book that I just could not believe. It said that even the hairs on your head have all been counted.

"Jesus was preparing his followers to go out in the world to tell people about Him. He knew that it was not going to be easy. He promised them that it would not matter if they were shy or felt like a dummy doing it. God would give them the words to say, kind of like a ventriloquist who makes the mouth of his puppet move, but is really the one doing the talking."

I moved my fingers and thumb like a talking hand that looked at me and back at them as I said it.

"How are you doing down there?" I asked the brothers who were still working on their project. The little brother was still standing as still as a rock, and his older brother was systematically dividing hairs and counting. He shook his head vehemently, clearly annoyed at my interruption. "Oops, sorry," I whispered.

"Well, I'll just go on with my story then," I said, looking up. "Anyway, Jesus went on to tell his disciples that even with God speaking through them, some people would not want to hear what they had to say and would try to stop them. He told them that even if bad things happened to them because they told others that they believed Jesus was sent by God to save them, God would know about it.

"Even if we don't understand why bad things happen, we just have to trust Him. There are many stories in The Book where a bad thing happens; then something good comes from it.

"For example, Joseph was beaten and sold as a slave by his brothers and then became the king's highest official in Egypt. Years later, he was in the right place at the right time to be able to save his whole family from dying of hunger when there was no food. God was the only one who knew things would turn out that way.

"Even if bad things happen to you, 'Jesus said [paraphrasing] *keep remembering that each of us is so important to God that He even knows how many hairs there are on our heads.*'

"Are you finished yet?" I asked the counter.

"No," he sighed in exasperation, "and you just made me lose my place."

"Would it help if the other kids came up and helped?" Little brother looked panic-stricken at the thought of a dozen pairs of hands pawing through his scalp.

The kids came to his rescue.

"I don't think that would work either."

"We would just get in each other's way."

"How would we know if somebody else had already counted one of the hairs we were counting?"

"It would be too confusing."

"What if we started with somebody with less hair, maybe like Roy?" I asked, pointing back to where the prematurely balding youth leader sat. He wasn't too thrilled.

"I still don't think it would work," one of the others decided, "It's just too hard."

"Well, how does God do it then?" I puzzled.

The consensus of shrugs in the group was mingled with variations on the same theme, "Because He is God, and I am not." What a wise little bunch!

"Well, it boggles my mind how He can do it," I said shaking my head, "but I just remembered something else I read in The Book. The things that God knows that I don't would outnumber the grains of sand.

"Hey!" I snapped my fingers, excitedly, "I just had a thought. How many of you like to go to the beach?" Everybody brightened at the notion and began to regal me with tales of their favorite sandy shores. "Well," I interrupted, "have you ever tried to count the grains of sand while you were there?"

That very thought triggered a chorus of laughter from the entire room.

"What is so funny about that?" I asked, innocently. "If we got enough people involved all over the world, and we worked together for say, a few million years, couldn't we count them? If we knew how many there were, we could begin to understand *just how BIG God is* and how amazing it is that a God that big would even know how many hairs I have on my head. How can God do that? It makes my brain hurt just thinking about it!"

I held my head in my hands.

The consensus of exasperated shrugs in the group this time was like an innocent repeat: "We already told you, don't you get it??" Still mingled with variations on the same theme, it got their point across to what they perceived as so obvious, I had to be a complete dunce not to get it!

"Because He is God, and I am not." What a wise little bunch!

But even the hairs of your head are all counted. (Matthew 10:30)

As for you, you meant evil against me, but God meant it for good in order to bring about this present result, to keep many people alive. (Genesis 50:20)

How precious also are Your thoughts for me, God! How vast is the sum of them! Were I to count them, they would outnumber the sand. (Psalm 139:17-18a)

Chapter
SIX
MY HEIRLOOM GLOBE

"Tell me the names of places you've traveled!" I prompted my attentive flock and was rewarded with a wave from most of them and shouts naming their destinations. Several children one-upped that contest by pronouncing foreign destinations they had learned playing *Where in the World Is Carmen Sandiego?*

"Last night my kids were working on their homework when my daughter said she needed a globe but was sure they were expensive at the mall.

"Then I pointed to the top of our eight-foot bookshelf where the heirloom globe from my childhood sat, gathering dust. I had wanted a globe when I was about her age and had been thrilled to find one under the Christmas tree that year."

As the kids tried to stay out of my way, I did my best to recreate the fancy dancing I had done to get the globe down from its perch—wading across the couch to the end table, finally standing on my tiptoes and snagging a corner of its base without knocking over the table lamp. The kids giggled as I lurched across the chancel and retrieved my heirloom globe from behind the lectern.

"Last night, I took it outside to blow most of the dust off of it, and then finished removing the rest of the grime with a damp cloth." I wiped the globe with a cloth and with a puff of air, recreated my cleaning project. "I think I did a pretty good job, don't you?" I twirled the globe, revealing my treasure. "Plus, I was pretty proud of myself for having avoided the cost of a new one." My little audience nodded like they were emptying their own piggy banks.

"Ahh," I nodded, raising a finger, "but there is a whole lot more to the story."

The kids leaned forward expectantly.

"So, I handed my globe to my daughter and headed off to the kitchen when not two minutes later, I heard a chorus of chortles from the family room. Of course, I did what your moms would do.

" 'No TV until after dinner!' I called out.

" 'It's not on. We're studying,' came the reply.

" 'Yeah, right. Is your homework that funny?'

" 'It is *now*.' More laughter ensued. Finally, they appeared in the kitchen doorway, globe in hand. 'Guess what?'

" 'What? Did you break it? I told you it was kind of old.'

" 'No, we didn't break it, but we might as well have.' More giggles, and then the *gotcha*!

" 'Mom, these countries don't exist anymore,' they informed me.

I looked out over the congregation and saw a lot of curious faces.

Then I gave the globe a final spin for emphasis and proceeded to pass on the education my children had given their clueless mom.

"Just for starts, look up *Ceylon*, or *Formosa*, or a real biggy— *USSR*. It is amazing how many changes have taken place, just in my lifetime," I marveled as I let the whirling globe drift slowly to a stop. "One name hasn't changed, however, and it never will.

"Before Moses led his captive people out of Egypt on a long, amazing journey across the wilderness, he had a rather strange conversation with God himself. Things got a little weird when a burning bush started talking to him—but when he realized God was in the bush, he was either brave enough to stay and listen or too scared to move.

"I have to tell you, I may be brave enough to face a lot of things, but if a shrub in my yard struck up a conversation with me, I think

I would probably faint on the spot. In fact, just thinking about it makes me woozy."

When I put my hand to my forehead and asked the group if they would catch me when I passed out, all traces of imagined heroics vanished.

"Whew!" I said, as I rallied, and their concern dissolved. "Ok, moving on. God told him to go back to Egypt and rescue His chosen people! Moses was a wanted fugitive in Egypt, however, and was not particularly anxious to go back there. God reminded him that He was the God of his famous ancestors—the very Lord Moses had vowed to serve and that He would be completely in charge of this mission. Moses just had to agree to be His missionary.

"Eventually, Moses realized he should probably stop arguing with a Supreme being who could keep a blazing fire going in a mere bush and yet not burn it up. He gave in.

"When he asked God who he should tell the people had spoken with him, God gave him an answer that was as timeless as He is. 'I AM.'

"That way, He would remain current no matter what puny territorial adjustments man made throughout history. Borders may move, civilizations come and go, but God remains the same forever. The Book makes it very clear that He is not, and never will be, 'I WAS.' "

I reminded my little audience of a bulletin board in our church foyer prominently displaying a map of the world. On each side are pictures of the missionaries we support and pray for. Pieces of yarn stretch from each picture to the spot in the world where these courageous families are serving.

"Our own missionaries set out on long journeys to dangerous places and, someday, maybe you will too. You might end up in a land where the people look different, and you can't even understand their language. The people there might wear different clothes. Their customs and food might be *really* different."

"The point is, it doesn't matter where you end up in life, the same neighborhood you live in now or a distant country far away. As you go out into the world, wherever your travels take you, tell them I AM has sent you."

Then Moses said to God, "Behold, I am going to the sons of Israel, and I will say to them, 'The God of your fathers has sent me to you.' Now they may say to me, 'What is His name?' What shall I say to them?" And God said to Moses, "I AM WHO I AM"; and He said, "This is what you shall say to the sons of Israel: 'I AM has sent me to you.'" (Exodus 3:13-14)

This is My name forever, and this is the name for all generations to use to call upon Me. (Exodus 3:15b)

Chapter
SEVEN

SUPERHERO

"I have to tell you," I said kneeling down so I was at eye-level with my weekly group, "Every morning, I get up, and I sit in traffic for almost an hour to get to the office where I work. Every day there is a new pile of papers on my desk to go through. At the end of every day, I get in my car and sit in traffic for another hour to drive home.

"It doesn't sound very exciting, does it?" I looked out at the congregation. "Does anyone out there have a really exciting job they do all week that they would like to trade for mine?" Nobody volunteered.

"Does anyone out there have their own boring job that they do all week?" Almost every hand in the room went up.

I looked back at the children. "Who can tell me about Superman?" They all started talking at once, but finally conceded the floor to their spokesman who gave me a detailed overview.

"Yes, he is pretty impressive all right," I interrupted, "What does he do when he is *not* being Superman?"

"He is a newspaper reporter named Clark Kent," the kids informed me.

"But how come no one knows he is Superman?"

One of the adults who, obviously, grew up watching the original version of the story answered, "because he is mild-mannered."

I laughed and nodded, "Do you kids know what mild-mannered means?"

They shrugged.

"It means he was very quiet and ordinary and, besides, his job was sooooo boring that no one suspected that he was really a superhero.

"One day when I was at my ordinary job, someone I worked with started telling me she had a 'spirit guide' and asked me if I was interested in having my own spirit guide.

"When I told her I didn't need one, she launched into telling me all the benefits she got from this relationship. While she was doing that, the Holy Spirit of God that I rely on to guide me, reminded me that The Book is very explicit that those spirit guides are not from God and that we are not to have anything to do with them.

"At that point, do you know what happened to me?" I asked, lowering my voice mysteriously.

My wide-eyed listeners shook their heads as I stood up. They were getting used to my weird surprises.

Letting my arms out of the sleeves of my coat and releasing all but the top button, I threw it back over my shoulders like a cape and revealed a large silver "S" on the chest of my shirt.

"Suddenly, I stopped being just another person with a boring job." With my hands on my hips, I announced, "I became SUPER SANDIE."

They all giggled. "No, seriously, I really did," I said, but I still had to wait a few minutes for them to stop laughing before I could continue.

"Well, I was not able to leap tall buildings in a single bound, but do you know what I was able to do?" They hushed, expectantly.

"I was able to speak up and say boldly, 'I don't need a spirit guide because I already have the Holy Spirit in me. Why would I want some puny spirit to guide me when I can have the most powerful

Spirit of all, whenever I need it?'

"It was amazing how quickly her spirit guide paled to my True Guide.

"The Book says that Jesus told his disciples they would receive the Holy Spirit's POWER to be His witnesses all over the world. Do you realize that even today, the most ordinary person with the most boring job can suddenly be filled with the supernatural power of God's Holy Spirit: THE SAME POWER to do what those who believe that Jesus was God's Son and our Savior could do then, TELL OTHERS ABOUT IT!"

I turned to the whole congregation and said, "If you see a car accident, what does the police report call you?"

"*A witness*," everyone in the room said in unison.

"That's right. You witnessed it and you can't unsee what you saw."

Turning back to the kids, I said, "Jesus told his disciples, 'You SHALL BE my witnesses.' He was telling them, you saw me DIE, and you saw me come back to LIFE, and you can't unsee it. Then, as He started rising up into the clouds, his last words were to tell them they would be given supernatural power to tell everyone, everywhere, WHAT THEY HAD WITNESSED.

I pointed to the big silver S on my shirt and reminded the group, "Superman always had to duck into a phone booth and take his boring, ordinary clothes off to uncover his exclusive Superman clothes before he was ready to fly off to use his special superpower to 'save the day.'

"The Holy Spirit's power just comes on you when you need it. You don't have to DO anything but wait for it. It will give you all the power you need to be a champion for God's cause."

I stretched out one fist and held the other to my chest like Superman does when he is flying and shouted, "You will become a superhero for Jesus, the One that even DEATH had no power over!"

Do not turn to mediums or spiritists; do not seek them out to be defiled by them. I am the LORD your God. (Leviticus 19:31)

But the Spirit explicitly says that in later times some will fall away from the faith, paying attention to deceitful spirits and teachings of demons... (1 Timothy 4:1)

But you will receive power when the Holy Spirit has come upon you; and you shall be My witnesses both in Jerusalem and in all Judea, and Samaria, and as far as the remotest part of the earth. (Acts 1:8)

Chapter
EIGHT

GUESSING GAME

"Animal, Mineral, Vegetable," and then I paused to insert "or Spiritual?" "We're going to play a game of charades. The kids and I are going to act out a few things, and the congregation has to try to guess what it is."

I passed out several slips of paper to some of the older kids, while instructing the congregation, "Your one hint is that it is something *spiritual*. Is everyone ready? OK kids, everybody line up and hold hands. Whatever you do, promise you will not let go."

I called a cute little girl to the head of the line. "Now, all of us are going to shut our eyes. No peeking, except our leader, Faith. Faith, would you please lead all of us over to the other side of the room where your grandma is sitting?" The little ones gamely struggled forward with encouragement not to let go, even if the whole group had to slow down to wind around a chair, or if somebody stumbled. Their little eyes were dramatically scrunched shut. "Any guesses?" I prompted.

"A snake with the hiccoughs?" ventured one brave competitor.

"Remember, the hint was something *spiritual*, not *animal*," I reminded. There were a few more baffled stabs at the answer, and finally, they admitted defeat. I beckoned to the girl holding the slip of paper containing the first answer and she read, "*For we walk by faith, not by sight.*" (2 Corinthians 5:7)

"See, we all shut our eyes and let Faith lead us across the room.

Wanna play again?" Everyone leaned forward in their seats. I took that for a *yes.*

I whispered something in Faith's ear who gave me a quick nod, and then sorted through the group until she found her little brother. With utmost tenderness she wrapped her arms around him and, giving him a kiss on the cheek, she proceeded to hug the stuffing out of him. It looked like a Norman Rockwell picture and there were a lot of "oohs," but no guesses. I looked around the room.

"Why is Faith doing that?" I finally asked. The answer was a unanimous chorus of "She loves him!" Had I held up a cue card, it could not have been more orchestrated. "You won that round!" I commended them, and I nodded to the youngster holding the slip of paper with the second answer, "*. . . the only thing that counts is faith expressing itself through love*" (Galatians 5:6b, NIV).

"OK, last one." I sent Faith up the steps toward the altar and dispatched the other children back to their seats. When she turned to face the congregation, she realized that no one had followed her up there. She gave me an inquisitive look but, little ham that she was, made no move to leave. The room was quiet for a good half minute, and then the pastor began to smile. He was just about to deliver his annual Reformation sermon which gave him all the hints he needed.

"I think I have it," he said. "Could it be *Sola Vide*, Martin Luther's concept of FAITH ALONE?

"Bravo! Good call," I agreed. "She is demonstrating faith alone."

"Hmm," he responded, shaking his head sadly. "I was kind of hoping I was wrong, because she just upstaged a third of my sermon." The congregation laughed.

They don't say a picture is worth a thousand words for nothing. We can grasp the concept of *faith alone* by hearing someone theologize and expound on it, but seeing Faith standing there alone, looking, well, winsome, makes every heart long for it.

Unfortunately, we can't see faith.

The Book defines faith as *"being sure of what we hope for and certain of what we do not see"* (Hebrews 11:1, NIV). Yes, walking by faith would come a lot easier if we could put an adorable face to it, but our real problem is shutting our eyes and still seeing that face. Faith is a noun (look it up). We don't have to do anything more than ALLOW ourselves to be led.

The Book says that we are to *"use the amount of faith that we have been given."* (Romans 12:3, paraphrased). It also says faith *"is the gift of God"* (Ephesians 2:8b).

How often I have heard someone say, "My faith is too small," or "I don't have enough faith." Does that mean that we can blame God for our lack of faith? *It is God's fault! He did not give me enough faith to do such and such.*

Picture again, the straggling little band of children being led forward by Faith. The kids all promised they would not peek, and they would not let go. Think of the one who is in the line right behind Faith as having "a lot of faith," and the one at the end of the line as having "little faith." Does that mean that the one with little faith cannot get to the same place as the ones further up the line? Obviously, the answer is "No, not if the one on the end does not let go."

How about someone in the middle? If something, or someone, causes that one to stumble, and their grip on the hand in front of them is lost, that person can lead everyone behind them down the wrong path. The important thing is NEVER EVER let go! Never break faith with the faithful so that those who are encouraging you, and those who are being encouraged by you, continue to follow wherever faith leads.

The person in front of the one who stumbles (one who has more faith) must get a tighter grip and patiently hold the chain together between the ones who are both leading and following. Think of that example as having your faith STRETCHED. It may hurt a little but, in the long run, it is good for you, and it is a beautiful example of faith expressing itself through love.

Sometimes, when I am playing with my granddaughter, I will shut my eyes and let her lead me. I don't know where we are going, but I love her so much that I am willing to go where she drags me, just because it brings her such glee to have me "in her power."

How much great joy it must it bring our heavenly Father to have us love Him so much that we are willing, by faith, to put ourselves "in His power" and blindly follow where He leads.

Trust in the LORD *with all your heart and lean not on your own understanding; in all your ways acknowledge him, and he will make your paths straight.* (Proverbs 3:5-6)

Chapter NINE

FEEDBACK

One morning, when the worship leader drifted away from his microphone to make an adjustment on his music stand, an ear-piercing electronic shriek filled the sanctuary. The entire congregation covered their ears and yelped in pain.

Quickly, his head snapped back to its proper place, directly in front of the microphone, and the noise stopped.

As I called the children forward that morning, I thanked the worship leader for the special message he had just given us.

He looked at me, curiously, as I wrapped my hand around his microphone stand and asked the kids what they thought of the horrible sound we had heard. Even the youngest ones expressed their distaste for what had happened.

"Would you like to hear it again?" I asked, reaching for the microphone.

"NO!" bellowed the entire congregation.

"Once was MORE than enough!"

"You don't wear a hearing aid, so you have no idea how painful that was," explained one of the older members.

"Sorry about that," the worship leader said, contritely, "My bad."

"Besides," chimed in a disconnected voice from up in the loft where the mixing board resided, "you can't do it again. I turned all the microphones off."

All the little heads toggled back and forth at each new remark.

"It appears I am unanimously outvoted." I conceded and, putting on my best man-on-the-street interview face, I turned back to the worship leader.

"Excuse me sir, can you tell us, in your own words, what caused this accident in which so many innocent people were injured?"

"The mics are tilted toward the speakers on the back wall where the music comes through," he said playing along. "If my mic is aimed directly at one of the speakers, without my head between them you get what we call feedback, or distortion."

"So, if you had put your hand over your mic when you moved your head away it wouldn't have happened?" I reasoned, logically.

"Well, not exactly," he went on. "Sometimes, if you cover the mic with your hand, it will also distort."

"So, help me out here, sir. You can't *uncover* it, and you can't *cover* it? That sounds like a no-win situation. How do you keep the shriek from happening?"

The kids were scratching their heads and frowning at him, clearly enjoying the debate.

"It isn't easy," he laughed, "but you learn the hard way what you can and can't do. I have had to endure a lot of ear-splitting consequences for not being in the right position to keep it from happening during our rehearsals."

"We all have," the rest of the team agreed.

"What about the pastor?" one youngster observed, pointing to the pulpit mic.

"You're right! What about you, pastor? I asked.

"I've had to learn to keep my head between the microphone and the speaker and my mouth about a thumb's distance from the mic screen." He agreed, demonstrating with his fist. "In fact, the soundman spent a great deal of time adjusting my microphone to get the best possible levels for everyone to be able to understand me clearly: Not too loud, not too soft, not too much bass, and not too much treble."

"Oh, you'd be surprised what I can do," came the soundman's voice from the loft. He flipped the mixing board's *reverb* on briefly so that what he was telling us through his microphone came out with an annoying echo (echo echo). The kids loved it!

"So, let me see if I got this straight," I said, summarizing the list on my fingers: "You have to stay fixed in the right position; you can't move off-center or try to muffle it with your hand for even a second."

"That's pretty much it," the soundman said. "The system gives you its feedback to tell you it doesn't like what you're doing. The only way to fix it, if you don't get back into the right position, is for me to turn the microphone off."

"Can you turn the pastor off if he preaches too long?" asked a voice from the crowd. We all broke into laughter. With everyone in the room fully engaged, it wasn't hard to nudge us toward a spiritual conclusion.

"God does not want us to *distort* what we say to others about Him.

"The Book gives us *feedback* to remind us that the best way to guard against distorting the Word of God is to make sure we stay focused on His Truth. We could call it *God's Positioning System!*"

I began listing them with my fingers again.

"Our praises must be directed to Him alone; the Word delivered by us must be centered on Him; and, just like the painful distortion we felt this morning, if we distort God's Word, it will hurt those who are listening.

"Sadly, sometimes the damage it does isn't just temporary. It can be so permanent it is ETERNAL." I paused and let that sink in.

"Just picture God putting His hands over his ears like we did and yelling, 'SHUT UP!' "

Everyone snickered at the sacrilegious image, but the

soundman one-upped me.

"Could be worse, ya know," he said from the loft, turning his volume up and flipping the reverb back on. In a thundering echo, we heard a God-like voice say, "I can also SHUT YOU DOWN!"

Even I couldn't think of another line to follow that!

Pay close attention to yourself and to the teaching; persevere in these things, for as you do this you will save both yourself and those who hear you. (1Timothy 4:16)

We have renounced the things hidden because of shame, not walking in trickery nor distorting the word of God, but by the open proclamation of the truth commending ourselves to every person's conscience in the sight of God. (2 Corinthians 4:2)

Chapter TEN

HOW IT ENDS

"Who is the *Light of the world*?" I asked the kids gathered before me at the front of the church.

"JESUS!" they chorused in unison.

"That's right," I nodded, as I lit the candle I was holding.

"Jesus came not only to be our *Savior*, but to light the Way for us in a world dark with sin." All eyes were riveted on the tiny flame.

"But when the soldiers came and arrested Jesus in the Garden of Gethsemane, He instructed Peter not to fight back, and His enemies dragged Jesus away." My audience fidgeted nervously, obviously concerned about what was to come. "Within minutes, their Light was gone." I blew out the candle. "I'm sure Peter thought it was all over."

But my talk was not. The little wick sizzled and then suddenly the flame reappeared. The kids giggled as my mouth dropped open.

"Maybe it's not all over! In fact, The Book tells us that Peter followed the crowd that had taken Jesus because he wanted to see how it would end.

"Peter ends up being questioned by people around the fire in the temple courtyard." My voice was now hushed. The children leaned in to learn more. "Who remembers what happened next?"

One little voice said quietly, "He said he didn't know him and then a rooster crowed," which was enough to set off a crowing contest among the boys.

"Right again!" I applauded, "and because Jesus had already warned him about this, I am sure Peter felt terrible. When Jesus turned and looked right at Peter, I think Peter thought it was all over!!" I blew the candle out again.

This time they knew it was a trick candle, so they told me, "No, it's not over!" Sure enough, the little flame struggled back to life.

I smiled.

"Over the next few days things looked pretty hopeless. They whipped Jesus. They stabbed a painful wreath of thorns on his head. They nailed him to a cross where he hung for hours in pain. At each new horrible thing they did to Jesus, Peter probably thought, *It has to be over now. How much more can He take*?"

"Then Jesus died." The children looked down sadly. "The Book says that at that exact moment, even the light of the sun went out at the brightest time of the day." I blew the candle out again and the children watched in anticipation.

Again the candle flickered to life, and my voice went up a notch as the familiar story's suspense built.

"Then they took the Light of the world down from the cross, put Him in a dark cave, and rolled a huge boulder over the mouth of His tomb." I motioned that finale with my free hand and then paused. "And that," I said with a nod, "is the end of the story." I blew the candle and concluded, "You can all go back to your seats."

"No!" they chortled loudly, pointing at the feisty little candle. "Look, it came back to life again!"

"Well, how about that!" I exclaimed in surprise. "The Light of the world came back to life!" Now my congregation of kids relaxed and smiled.

"What about Peter? Remember him? After Jesus came back to life, Mary talked to Him in the cemetery and then ran to tell Peter the Good News.

"Peter, who had wanted to see how the story would end, found it never *did* end! The Light has shined in the darkness, the darkness has not overcome Him, and never will!"

All eyes focused on the tiny candle that continued to glow. I hoped the gospel light burned as brightly in all our hearts. The light continued on even after the children ran back to their seats and burned on through the service. Nothing could extinguish it. And when the last hymn was sung, I carried the candle out the door of the church into a world badly in need of the Light of the World.

So Jesus said to Peter, "Put the sword into the sheath; the cup which the Father has given Me, am I not to drink it?" (John 18:11)

But Peter was following Him at a distance, as far as the courtyard of the high priest, and he came inside and sat down with the officers to see the outcome. (Matthew 26:58)

And then the Lord turned and looked at Peter. And Peter remembered the word of the Lord, how He had told him, "Before a rooster crows today, you will deny Me three times." (Luke 22:61)

When the sixth hour came, darkness fell over the whole land until the ninth hour. (Mark 15:33)

The light shines in the darkness, and the darkness has not overcome it. (John 1:5, NIV)

"THEY STABBED A PAINFUL WREATH OF THORNS
ON HIS HEAD."

Chapter
ELEVEN

DIED FOR YOU

Jim Harper and I rehearsed a special children's presentation for Easter but no amount of practice prepared us for what happened that Sunday morning. The kids had their own ideas!

After his warm welcome, the children gathered around him.

"We are here to celebrate Easter!" he smiled at his entourage.

"I'm here!" I announced, as I bounded into the room disguised as the Easter Bunny.

"The celebration can now begin." I swung my Easter basket happily. Jim's scathing look tipped the children off that he was not happy to see me.

"Well, as I was saying before we were interrupted, today is Easter," he continued.

"I know, I know. Here comes my favorite part. Go ahead, tell 'em, tell 'em!"

Again, he glared at me as he continued, "Remember how we told you at the Good Friday service that Jesus died for you?"

"What?!!" I sputtered, "That's not right! *I* dyed for you!"

All of the little heads swiveled in my direction. "You did not," they chorused.

"I did so," I countered, fuzzy paws on hips. "Before I came along, there were only white eggs and maybe a few brown eggs. I dyed them pink. I dyed them blue. I dyed them green. I dyed them purple! I dyed them for you! *I* dyed for you."

"*That's* not the kind of *die* we are talking about," Hunter corrected, impatiently.

"It isn't?" I frowned, raising my paws upward. "What kind of dye are you talking about?"

"Like DEAD," she explained. The weight of her words hung heavy in the church.

"Ewwwh!" I shrank back at the very thought.

"Yes," said Jim, who had stood fascinated by this unscripted exchange between the kids and the bunny, "but remember, He didn't STAY dead. He came to life again on Easter, or what we call Resurrection Day." Then turning to me, he added, "and we celebrate His triumph over sin and death, because He died for us."

I cocked my ears and tried to think of something profound to interject. Finally, the best I could come up with was "Huh?"

"Okay," he said, "pay attention." The kids watched our interchange as if it were a tennis match, but they were clearly cheering on Team Jim. "Jesus died on the cross for our sins, and He was raised from the dead on Easter. That's why we celebrate."

I wasn't working off a script anymore, just improvising as one big rabbit.

"So, you mean I have no value?" I asked, incredulously.

"Oh no," he assured me, smiling. "You have a great deal of value. In fact, I'd like to have you for dinner."

"Oh goody," I brightened, as he hooked an arm through my paw and started walking down the aisle.

"By the way," he asked, stopping half-way out the door, "How do you feel about stew...maybe barbeque?"

We had scripted an interchange about the connection between the crucifixion and the resurrection, but the kids took it in a new direction. And it sure did our hearts good to know the kids knew how to separate the myth of the Easter bunny from the real meaning of our Easter celebration: Jesus is risen! He is risen indeed!

And being found in appearance as a man, He humbled Himself by becoming obedient to the point of death: death on a cross. (Philippians 2:8)

Do not be amazed; you are looking for Jesus the Nazarene, who has been crucified. He has risen; He is not here; see, here is the place where they laid Him. (Mark 16:6)

BONUS EASTER CHAPTER: HALLUCINATIONS AND HALLELUJAHS

Several years ago, my job included delivering legal documents to the county office for recording. Afterwards, I would treat myself to a mocha-to-go at the espresso stand by the elevator to the parking garage.

One day when I made the turn that would take me back to the freeway, my trip took a little detour from reality. I suddenly found myself driving down the street completely surrounded by . . . ELEPHANTS.

There they were, plodding along next to me, apparently oblivious to me and my car. *I am hallucinating,* I reasoned, shaking my head. About then I spilled some of the hot mocha on my knees, which was kind of a relief because the sudden pain reassured me that the elephants must be some kind of stress-induced fantasy. Just to make sure, I glanced in the rear-view mirror and began to breathe a little easier until I saw *something* resembling a broad hind end with a rope-like tail just disappearing around the corner of a building several blocks behind me.

When I reached my office, I blurted out the whole unbelievable episode to my coworkers, and their reactions were predictable. One of them sneered at my mental condition and rolled her eyes. Another interrupted to tell me something even more spectacular had happened to her once. One friend reminded me she had been telling me for quite some time that I needed a vacation. One named Gwen just listened quietly and, finally, shaking her head said, "I know it sounds crazy, but I think I believe you."

The next morning, I found a newspaper clipping with a photo of marching circus elephants sitting on my desk with a little note attached "FYI." The photo caption read as follows:

> Ringling Bros. and Barnum & Bailey Circus elephants amble along yester-
> day on the Pacific Avenue overpass from Everett Station to the Everett Events
> Center. The circus, which begins a four-day run today, is drawing fans as well
> as foes, who complain it is cruel to its animal stars.

(September 16, 2004)

Credit: Meryl Schenker, Seattle *Post-Intelligencer*

It had really happened. The circus had come to town!

I read how it was the carnys' job to walk the elephants from the circus train to the event center a few blocks away. Traffic had been detoured from the route they were taking but, somehow, I had, inadvertently, turned into it anyway. I was giddy with relief and couldn't wait to share the newspaper "proof" with everyone who thought I had finally gone over the edge.

Okay, I may have been smirking a bit as my apologetic associates came up to see what newspaper clipping I was pinning to the office message board. As I stared at the evidence they were shaking their heads at, I couldn't help but think that this may have been how Mary felt when, after seeing the *risen* Jesus in the garden, returned to the disciples.

She too was probably wondering if she had actually seen what she thought she had seen. Maybe she even considered keeping it to herself, but then, suddenly found herself blurting out the incredibly unbelievable news.

The disciples' reactions, like my coworkers, ranged from ridicule to rapture. Some, like Peter and John, followed her to check out her story. Some, like Thomas, doubted to the point of saying that they needed tangible proof. He said he was not going to fall for Mary's unbelievable story unless he could actually touch the wounds Jesus had gotten when He was crucified. Today, Thomas probably would say he wasn't going to believe my outlandish story unless he got to touch the elephant!

I wonder what the outcome would have been if a cub scribe for the Jerusalem Post had been hanging out in the garden looking for an exclusive scoop. He could have penned an article verifying the sightings in the Garden and given poor Mary the credibility she deserved with a bold headline in the next edition. The Good News of Salvation would most likely have gotten off to a different start, but it seems God is more interested in what inquiring *hearts* want to know than inquiring *minds*.

Few believed *my* story. It took a newspaper article to bring confirmation. Thousands of years later we have confirmation in THE BOOK, what today's writers, radio and film producers have unapologetically called THE GREATEST STORY EVER TOLD.

Jesus, our Risen Savior promised He would return to take us with Him and, as incredibly unbelievable as it sounds—it will happen!

There may have been no breaking news headline at the resurrection of Jesus but there is a glorious day coming when every eye will see Him return with trumpet fanfare and archangels and enough commotion to raise the dead and no more questions in any mind!

Thinking that He was the gardener, she said to Him, "Sir, if you have carried Him away, tell me where you put Him, and I will take Him away." Jesus *said to her, "Mary!" She turned and *said to Him in Hebrew, "Rabboni!" (which means, Teacher). Jesus said to her, "Stop clinging to Me, for I have not yet ascended to the Father; but go to My brothers and say to them, 'I am ascending to My Father and your Father, and My God and your God.'" (John 20:15–17)

For the Lord Himself will descend from heaven with a shout, with the voice of the archangel and with the trumpet of God, and the dead in Christ will rise first. Then we who are alive and remain, will be caught up together with them in the clouds to meet the Lord in the air, and so we will always be with the Lord. (1 Thessalonians 4:16-17)

Chapter
TWELVE

EASY INSTRUCTIONS

"Attention please! I have some very important instructions everyone needs to know." The kids in the congregation scrambled quickly to the front of the church.

"Some of you may already know how to do this, and you can help those who don't, so please listen carefully while I explain." The children huddled before me became a sea of rapt expressions. The adults in the congregation smiled, indulgently.

"Step One: Grasp Unit B with the extremity of the inferior limb. Utilizing a counter clockwise motion, circumscribe Unit B with Unit A until the furthest point of Unit A is exposed."

I paused and glanced up. The faces, old and young, seemed frozen.

"Step 2: Oppose the furthest points of Unit A and Unit B until they are equal."

I peeked over my glasses but saw no one following directions.

"OK then, moving on." I continued.

"Step 3: Apply firm tension to Unit B while concurrently looping the index digit of the extremity of the inferior limb through Unit A and immediately bind the two units together at the base with the extremity of the dominant limb." I took a deep breath after that run-on sentence. Afraid to look up, I raised my voice slightly for emphasis and went on.

"Step 4: Employing a clock-wise motion, completely circum-scribe Unit A and Unit B and propel a plicature of Unit B through the orifice created by this exercise with the index digit of the extremity of the inferior limb."

By this time, one little boy was picking his nose, and his sister was trying to capture his hand. A few children shrugged at their parents in the congregation and when I scanned the adults, I saw nothing but frowns.

"Step 5: Bind all aspects of Units A & B together at their base with the opposable digit of the extremity of the inferior limb."

None of the children were looking at me anymore. They fidget-ed and whispered. I better not dally.

"Step 6: FINALLY, grasp the plicature of Unit A between the op-posable and index digits of the extremity of the dominant limb, and the plicature of Unit B between the opposable and index dig-its of the extremity of the inferior limb, and oppose their furthest points until they are equal." I spoke faster and faster to arrive at the conclusion.

"There! Any questions" I didn't wait for an answer. "None?" I asked. "Does anyone want to help demonstrate?" Even the few who thought they might have gotten it were reluctant to come for-ward. I surveyed my group and zeroed in on a girl proudly wearing brand new shoes with lights on the sides and reached over to pull her shoelace free.

"Very slowly re-tie your shoes." As she did so, I repeated the in-structions I'd given earlier. Everyone leaned forward to watch in-tently, applauding when we were finished.

Then I beckoned to the toddler with the nose fixation whose shoelace already dangled conveniently free. His mother gasped, "He can't tie his shoelaces yet."

"No big deal," I countered, "he can just follow along as I read him the instructions." She looked at me like I had lost my mind.

"You've got to be kidding! Even I could not understand those instructions."

I gave the "what she said" nods in the crowd a slow going over.

"Hmmm. Well then, I guess we just have to go to Plan B."

"Bill, can you join us for a few minutes?" I smiled as my husband came forward. "We will see if *his* way of teaching our children to tie their shoes still works."

Bill took the little boy in his lap, with one chubby leg on his knee, and took the shoestrings in his hands.

"This is a tree" he announced, holding up one of the strings, "and here comes a rabbit," he said hopping the other string toward it. "The rabbit goes around the tree and down into his hole. Then he POPS up out of his hole and leaps up in the air." Bill tightened the strings, holding them together like an ear, and did a bunny nose wiggle at the kids. "Pretty soon, the rabbit scampers around the tree again and back down in his hole. Do you think we will see him again?" By this time, the whole group was hanging all over him, watching expectantly. "Wait, is that another ear I see?" The kids all clapped to see a loop emerging from the hole. "This time, two birds see him POP out of his hole. They swoop down and pull on the rabbit's ears. There!" he said as he pulled the loops tight. "All tied!"

He was rewarded with a big smile from the youngster followed by "me do, me do."

"Jesus is called Teacher sixty times in The Book but sometimes His disciples had as much trouble understanding His instructions as you did understanding mine. Sometimes He had to break down His lesson in simple terms even a child could understand," I pointed to Bill and the child still nestled in his lap.

"In The Book, Jesus used parables to get his point across but, occasionally, even His story example seemed to go right over their heads." I said waving my hand over my head. "Jesus patiently explained and *showed* them, like Bill did, except He did it by the life He lived and things He did. They may not have understood it quickly, or even easily but, one by one, they all got it." My little congregation smiled back at me and nodded.

"Just as someone taught you, by example, how to tie your shoes by an easily understood illustration like a rabbit hole," I winked at the kids and they smiled at Bill who wiggled his nose again, "Each of YOU can teach someone else by example and story."

I didn't stop there. "But I don't just mean how to tie shoes, you can follow what Jesus said to do and go out and teach others what Jesus taught.

"Jesus finished His earthly ministry saying, 'I did my part; now you know; now YOU go. Oh, and one last thing, I'll be here if you need help.' As they watched him ascending to heaven, he was making it very clear that it was not *game over*, it was *game on*."

Go, therefore, and make disciples of all the nations, baptizing them in the name of the Father and the Son and the Holy Spirit, teaching them to follow all that I commanded you; and behold, I am with you always, to the end of the age. (Matthew 28:19-20)

Chapter
THIRTEEN

BODYBUILDER

"I'm going to need lots of help this morning," I told the kids as I handed each of them a large envelope. Then I asked one of the older boys to take a couple more envelopes outside and put them on the porch. I delivered the last envelope to a family who was visiting that morning.

"OK, open your envelopes and let's see if we can build a body." I stood ready with a handful of metal fasteners as each of them pulled a simply illustrated cardboard body part out of the envelope they held.

"Does anybody have a head?" I asked, scanning my audience. One of them held up a round smiley face into which we inserted the fastener. "Who has a chest?" Another one held up the lumpy ribcage which had a heart-shaped cut-out. "Now we need some arms," I said as we fastened the chest to the head. One arm was handed over to me, and two kids with hands leaned forward, ready to be next. We fastened the one arm to the torso, followed by one of the hands. But then my smile faded and I had to apologize.

"I am so sorry," I told the youngster holding the other hand. "We can't use your hand because there is no arm to attach it to. You hang on to it, OK?" He waved the hand as if saying goodbye.

"Who has the hips?" Nobody did. "How about legs?" Both legs showed up, as well as one foot. We attached the foot to one of the legs and then stood up to survey our efforts. "Hmmm, we seem to be missing some important pieces. I must have forgotten something. Does anybody have a part I haven't collected yet?" Two ears were passed forward from the group, and we soon had them added to our growing body.

"Anything else?" The youngster still in possession of the lone hand held it up again. Like a group of engineers, we pondered the unfinished body.

"What do you think we should do?" I asked them. Several hands shot up, so I encouraged their input.

"Maybe there is an arm in one of the other envelopes," came one suggestion.

"What other envelopes?" I feigned ignorance.

"The ones outside," was the impatient answer.

"The one you gave to those people," said another.

"Well, let's find out," I said glancing up at the young couple several rows back who seemed intrigued by the project.

"Good morning visitors. We are glad you are worshiping with us today." I shook each of their hands. "We would like to get to know you better and hope that you make some new friends here." They both smiled, clearly not intimidated by the attention they were suddenly receiving.

"We have several programs to offer that you might find to your liking—Bible studies, a softball league, a prayer group—lots of things to meet your needs! Just as important, however, it appears that you have something WE need too."

"You mean this?" asked the man holding up his envelope.

"Yes!" came a chorus from my little bodybuilders, "Open it!"

He removed the hips from his envelope and handed it forward so I could now connect the chest to the legs. Everyone in the group was genuinely elated except for my sidekick still holding his disjointed hand.

"Wow," I said, looking toward the visitors. "Do you see how important you are to us? Without what you have to offer, we are so incomplete." Their eyes got wide as they suddenly realized that the project was more than just a children's game.

"Well, what should we do now?" I asked, shifting my focus back to the circle.

"We could see what is in the other envelopes," several of the children recommended.

"How do we do that?" I asked.

"We go out and bring them in," one of them volunteered.

"Go out there?" I pointed, shaking my head with a shiver. "It's cold outside, and I think it's raining. Are you sure we can't get along without them?" I asked, shrugging. "I mean how important can one arm and a foot be to our body?" I held up our physically challenged creation.

"Well, it is important to me!" said the one still holding the useless hand.

When I turned to ask if he wanted to bring in those envelopes, I saw he was already reaching for the doorknob.

Sure enough, to the cheering of my body builders, the cardboard body soon had its missing pieces.

"The Book tells us that 'the Body of Christ is not made up of *one* part, but of many.' God has arranged all the parts just as He wants them to be. As we saw when we put our body together, each of them was important to the other parts. I traced my hand along the fasteners. And without some of them, the other parts couldn't do their jobs." I moved the various body parts around like a puppet. "In fact, as we found out from the missing pieces, the hand can't say, 'I don't need an arm,' and the legs really needed the hips to be able to move." Dancing the body slightly brought on a round of giggles from the kids.

"Each person in this room is an indispensable part of the Body of Christ, and it is important for each of us to find our place.

Someone who can't carry a tune cannot say, 'because I am not part of the worship team, I am not part of the body.' If everybody was on the stage, where would the congregation be? Somebody who is crippled can't say, 'because my legs don't work, I do not belong to the body.' If everybody was busy running, where would the prayer ministry be?

"Sometimes a church body may seem lazy or weak, but it could just be missing some pieces that it needs to function. Each person you invite to worship with you, and each visitor who comes, might be an important piece that God will use to strengthen the Body."

Then I stopped to survey the body and frowned, shaking my head with concern.

"On the other hand, all of the parts might be accounted for, but the Body has a heart problem."

"The body we built is still missing the most important piece," I said, pointing to a heart-shaped cutout in the cardboard chest.

"But there are no more envelopes," several of the children protested.

"That is because the heart of the church is *God*, not a person," I said, reaching over to the altar and picking up a heart-shaped piece that lay at the foot of the cross. "The Book tells us that 'in Him we live and move and have our being.' We live in Christ, we move in the Spirit, and we have our being in God the Father. Without God at the center, it does not matter how well put together we are as a unit," I said, as I inserted the heart into its place at the very center of our body and patted it into place.

My industrious little band of bodybuilders seemed to grasp the weight of that final piece. Their tiny hands began to instinctively feel for their own heartbeats. I watched them nod and smile as they stood listening to the beating of their own life force and couldn't help but feel that, if they never lost that childish wonder, the earthly Body of Christ was in good hands.

For just as the body is one and yet has many parts, and all the parts of the body, though they are many, are one body, so also is Christ. (1 Corinthians 12:12)

For in Him we live and move and exist. (Acts 17:28a)

Chapter
FOURTEEN

THE TICKET

I asked the congregation if any of them had ever vacationed on a cruise ship as the kids were coming toward our usual spot on the steps below the altar. Several waved their hands and smiled.

"I don't know how your trip was but mine got off on kind of a disastrous start," I said, shaking my head.

I held out an 8-1/2x11 sheet of paper and began folding it as I told my tale.

"My cousin Susie invited us to join her family on an Alaskan cruise. When a glossy spiral-bound book arrived a few weeks later, I tossed it in my suitcase to read on the ship.

"I was puzzled when my cousin called asking if I had confirmed our reservations. 'Didn't you get a book in the mail?' she continued.

" 'Yes,' I said, 'I thought I would read it on the cruise.'

" 'Well,' she laughed, 'you won't be going on the cruise if you don't get it out and follow the directions. It has your ticket in it.'

"I dug the book out and, sure enough, a detailed list of instructions included calling a toll-free number to confirm our cabin and dining tables.

"I did not see anything in the book that remotely resembled a ticket.

"Finally, the departure day arrived, and we made our way to the dock. I was still uneasy about not seeing a ticket in the Cruise book that was now tucked in my purse.

"When it was my turn, I handed the agent at the counter my book with an apologetic shrug. 'This is all they sent. I sure hope something important didn't get lost in the mail.'

"Deftly, she flipped the book open to the page she wanted and tore the *ticket* from the book, 'No, it's all here.' We were on our way!

"I could not help but be reminded of another traveler who was on his way to heaven," I shared with my listeners. A man named David* found himself in a long line of people all waiting for an interview with St. Peter."

"David discovered a folded piece of paper in his hand and asked the person behind him what it might be."

" 'It's your ticket to heaven,' was the reply. 'Don't lose it. '

"A man named Saul,** who was just ahead of David, suddenly gasped and said, 'I don't seem to have one.'

"Saul felt in all his pockets and then turned in a panic.

"I don't suppose you could tear off some of your ticket for me? Maybe I could tell him it got damaged,' he said, frantically.

"Having lived a life helping his fellow man, David tore a strip from the folded ticket without hesitation."

I cut a similar strip from the folded paper I was holding and dropped it on the steps.

"The closer they got to heaven's gate," I continued, "the more agitated the hapless man grew. Finally, he turned around again to ask for more help.

" 'Maybe I didn't get enough,' Saul whined. 'Could you tear off some more?'

"Moved by his plea, David tore off another strip and handed it to him with a sympathetic smile.

"Mirroring the man's request, I cut off another strip of my folded paper and dropped it with the other pieces.

"Finally, they arrived at the gate. 'I'm sorry, but my ticket was accidentally damaged,' said Saul, as he dropped the pieces into St. Peter's hand.

'Well, let's have a look,' said St. Peter, and he began to unfold the pieces and lay them on the desk."

I did the same thing, laying my unfolded pieces together on the step. My kids were loving the story and leaned forward to see what I was doing.

" 'H . . . E . . . ,' he said. Saul relaxed visibly. St. Peter smiled at him and went on unfolding the pieces. 'L . . . L!' he finished, as the last piece was laid with the others. 'I'm sorry,' he said sadly, 'this is a ticket to hell, not heaven. I am afraid you are in the wrong line,' and he turned him away without further discussion."

As I laid the last 'L' in line with the first three letters, the kids were vocally amazed. "How did you do that?"

"That is so cool."

I smiled, sadly. "Yes, unfortunately, the fate of the man holding just those pieces was not so cool." Then I continued the story.

"When David, who had given up part of his ticket to try and help Saul, witnessed his terrible fate, he became uneasy. Sacrificing a portion of his own ticket now appeared to have been a very . . . unwise . . . decision."

As I enunciated those words, the kids nodded, sympathetically, as if they had experienced unwise decisions of their own.

"The good man handed what was left to St. Peter. 'I only have part of my ticket,' David shrugged apologetically. 'It's probably not going to be enough.'

"St. Peter began to open the folded paper. . . ." And so did I, as my curious kids watched with bated breaths.

"Finally, he held up what was left—the perfect shape of a cross. 'No,' he assured David with a smile, 'it's all here! Welcome Home!' "

Greeted with a din of "oohs" and "aahs", I held my perfect paper cross up for all to see. It was one of those incredible moments when all the pieces click into place in the minds of everyone in the room, and I was almost moved to tears by it.

As incredulous as it may seem, there is NOTHING ELSE that will gain our entry to God's heavenly kingdom. Man sold himself to Satan with that first sin at the dawn of creation. Jesus bought us back again with his death on the cross. You might say He purchased our ticket to heaven.

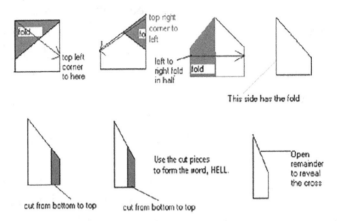

Diagram above by Donald Burns © 2005
Printed by permission of
SundaySchoolNetwork.com

"Worthy are You to take the scroll and to break its seals; for You were slaughtered, and You purchased people for God with Your blood from every tribe, language, people, and nation. (Revelation 5:9)

*David means *Beloved*
**Saul means *ask, inquire, borrow, beg*

Chapter
FIFTEEN
DON'T LEAVE HOME WITHOUT IT

"I was finally on my way with my Alaskan Cruise ticket—the real deal—in hand.

"As each of us boarded the cruise ship, our pictures were snapped and linked to a magnetically bar-coded, plastic card. I held mine up the next week for all to see."

So what? A plastic card, the children shrugged, collectively. *Don't know an adult who doesn't have one and don't really care until I get one of my own.*

Gamely, I went on, ignoring their indifference.

"We were **sternly** advised to have the card in our possession **at all times.**" I took a minute to make eye contact with each of them before I went on. "STERNLY ADVISED! HAVE THE CARD WITH YOU AT ALL TIMES!" I repeated. "The card will be used for all purchases and activities aboard ship; it will open your cabins; it will record your exit to each port of call, and it will secure each re-boarding."

And so, it did! It was like magic. Just whip that little card out, and the cruise ship was at my command! On-ship shopping? No problem. I probably had a few regrets later when I actually had to pay for the luxuries that caught my eye, but everybody else was splurging, so I thought at the time, *Why shouldn't I?* (Hmmm. . . a children's message on greed and envy would likely result from my decadent behavior, but from the look on the kids' faces, they weren't even liking this one.)

A skirmish was developing between the older boys in the back row who probably didn't want to be there, but their parents made them follow me up to the altar steps anyway.

I narrowed my eyes at the hooligans and thought to myself, *I am going to get you so good!* Having been raised in a house full of boys, I knew the next part of the story was going to suck them in.

"Shall we continue?" I asked, innocently. Thanks to the cleared throats of some of the fathers in the room, I was soon rewarded with some reluctant attention. I went on.

"On our last evening aboard, we were treated to a video of the cruise as it had been surreptitiously recorded from wall-mounted cameras about the ship. We even saw our own party laughing and talking as we strolled one of the corridors together.

"Not all the clips were quite that happy, however. One camera had recorded a man in his *underwear* returning a tray to the corridor for pick up, after he had enjoyed a room service meal."

At this point the boys' faces froze and I, suddenly, had their FULL attention.

"Now, as you know, underwear seldom has pockets so, obviously, there would be no place for his ID card. Besides, he wasn't really going anywhere. He was just going to set his empty tray in the corridor. So, you can imagine his shock and chagrin when his cabin door closed firmly behind him, and he realized that he now stood in the public corridor without his card, wearing nothing but his tighty-whities." Okay, I may have raised my voice when I said that, but it got the point across.

The boys were appalled! I was talking about men wearing nothing but their undershorts being embarrassed in public. Besides that, the girls in the group were starting to giggle and there was absolutely nothing the boys could do about it. They may even have been thinking about how humiliated they would be if they were caught in the Disney-inspired underwear they were wearing themselves. It was the escape valve the boys were hoping for when I continued this time.

"Without a doubt, the ignored instruction to have the card in his possession at all times *immediately* grew in importance; not to mention his profound embarrassment at seeing the episode re-lived on video before the jeering of the ship's entire assembly."

The boys' mouths all dropped at least an inch at this final stroke to masculine self-esteem, made worse by the decibel of the girls' taunting glee that was rising, considerably.

I shushed them with my hands but let almost a minute of si-lence go by to calm the mood before I got to the point.

"In your life, you may have a wallet full of plastic cards just like your parents may have now. If you learn how to use them respon-sibly, they will serve you well—but not only are they expensive to use, they are limited in what you can do with them.

"Salvation, or what gives us the right to live with God in His eternal kingdom, is very specific. We must have permission to en-ter. If a voice behind heaven's door asked me, 'Who are you and what do you want?' I would smile at the peep hole and say, 'My name is Sandie and Jesus sent me.' The Book tells us plainly that *there is no other way in. Our savior's name is the password* (Acts 4:12, paraphrased).The cross is the essential link between God and man. Trying to find another way would be like using any old card you happen to have in your wallet to try and board a cruise ship.

"By the same token, salvation may not seem all that important as we scurry about life. Some people genuinely believe they do not need it at all. Others are convinced that they have plenty of time before they are going to need it, so they put it off.

"Sooner or later, however, each of us will stand alone and *ex-posed* before the door to eternal life that only the Savior's name can open. Best not to leave home without it!

For if the word spoken through angels proved unalterable, and every violation and act of disobedience received a just punishment, how will we escape if we neglect so great a salvation? (Hebrews 2:2-3a)

And there is salvation in no one else; for there is no other name under heaven that has been given among mankind by which we must be saved. (Acts 4:12)

Chapter
SIXTEEN
THE INVISIBLE CAPTAIN

Wearing a flamboyant red scarf with a walkie talkie clipped to my waistband, I stood in front of my improvised row of half-pint cruise passengers.

"Before I introduce the Captain and crew, it is my privilege as Cruise Director to welcome you to our Alaskan Cruise opening gala. Let's start by giving you an overview of all you have to look forward to on this fun and food-filled journey."

Pretending to exert myself, I held up my two-inch thick cruise passenger guide. I flipped through it as if it were a flicker book while doing my best to vocally imitate the sound of a video on fast forward. About five seconds later, I dropped the book and began to clap, prompting them and a number of chuckling adults to do the same. "I hope you all enjoyed my informative presentation.

While they clapped, I snatched the 2-way radio up close to my ear for a moment and then held it to my mouth to respond. "Roger that. Over and out."

"Now," I shook my head sadly, "I have to apologize that you are not going to meet the Captain tonight, as I had promised. I just got word that his attention is needed elsewhere."

I unwound my red scarf and dropped my theatric role as I continued.

"In fact, due to varying circumstances, we never saw him during the entire week but by the end of the cruise, we had come to know him well. This is what we learned:

"First: He tended to each emergency personally. During the gala event, he had been supervising the airlift of a heart attack victim.

"Do you suppose that when the Captain was a child, he heard that story Jesus tells about the Good Shepherd in The Book?" Several of them nodded knowingly. "Maybe he remembered how the shepherd left the ninety-nine sheep to personally attend to the needs of the one lost lamb so he knew it was the right thing to do.

"Second: The Captain knew the way, even when we couldn't see it. There were several times during the journey when the fog and mist completely hid the ocean ahead; yet, the ship never even broke speed.

"Have you ever ridden in a car while it was raining?" Instead of a sea of raised hands, I got a sea of raised eyebrows. Every puzzled head in the room nodded. One of my little cruise passengers raised his hand to speak.

"One day our school bus driver told us to stop horsing around so she could concentrate on getting us home safe. It was really stormy and kind of scary."

"Did you get home safe?" I asked.

"Yep, our bus has a really good driver."

"Well, there you go then. Just so you know, The Book assures us that *nothing is hidden from God*. We should never despair when things are dark or when the road ahead seems unclear. God is a really REALLY good driver!

"Third: The Captain never veered off course, AND he never asked my opinion about it."

I stuck a very formal-looking Captain's hat on my head and gave a gruff imitation of a commanding officer's voice as I said "Mrs. Williams, would you mind coming up to the bridge? I have a few options I'd like your input on." Such an absurd notion brought on howls of glee.

"If that sounds silly, think how much more ridiculous it would be to second-guess the Creator of the Universe. According to The Book, *'God's thoughts and ways are higher than mine.'* What could I possibly offer except my complete trust?

"Finally, whenever 'This is your Captain speaking.' came over the intercom, all activity and conversation ceased until he was finished, as if someone had pressed a Pause button.

My startled audience wasn't sure how to react when I suddenly bellowed urgently, "This is your Captain speaking. Man your stations! I repeat, Man your stations!

"At the gala event we had been instructed to put our life jackets on and go to our assigned lifeboat stations if we heard the Captain give that order. So, everyone followed his orders and went straight to their stations with their life jackets on. Well, that is, *almost* everyone.

"One woman showed up carrying her purse instead of her life jacket. Dangling from her arm was also a shopping bag bearing the ship's logo. Instead of following the life jacket instructions, she had continued to dawdle in the ship's shopping mall.

"The ship's officer in charge scolded her loudly. He then assigned a crew member to take responsibility for her safety, should the need arise.

"And yes," I nodded, looking pointedly at the girls who had, just last week, been reveling in the boys' embarrassment at the man standing outside his room in his underwear, "she had to endure seeing her selfish behavior replayed . . ." I didn't need to finish that sentence. The smirking boys in my assembly finished it for me!

"The Book declares it is God's wish that *not any should perish* (2 Peter 3:9). He is disappointed and saddened when we disobey Him but still, when necessary, sends His ministering angels to serve those who will inherit salvation.

"No, I never got to see the Captain on my Alaskan Cruise, but I never doubted that he was there, nor that he had everything under complete control.

"We didn't need to see him to be able to enjoy all the things the manual said he was making available to us," I said holding up the Cruise manual.

Then I held my Bible aloft. "The Book says we can't see God either but everything He has created is showing us that He is there. While He is busy being the captain of our lives, He wants us to see Him and know Him in everything He is making possible for us."

What man among you, if he has a hundred sheep and has lost one of them, does not leave the other ninety-nine in the open pasture and go after the one that is lost, until he finds it? (Luke 15:4)

"For My thoughts are not your thoughts, nor are your ways My ways," declares the LORD. (Isaiah 55:9)

Are they not all ministering spirits, sent out to provide service for the sake of those who will inherit salvation? (Hebrews 1:14)

And we know that God causes all things to work together for good to those who love God, to those who are called according to His purpose. (Romans 8:28)

For since the creation of the world His invisible attributes, that is, His eternal power and divine nature, have been clearly perceived, being understood by what has been made, so that they are without excuse. (Romans 1:20)

Chapter
SEVENTEEN

ENTITLEMENT

This was my fourth tale with our church youngsters about my Alaskan cruise and I know my gang wondered if my 'caught in the act' competition was going to continue. I left them wondering as I told them, "I encountered two people on board who proved to be quite intriguing."

"The first thing I noticed about one elderly passenger was that the ship's staff called her by name, and SHE knew their names! She ambled about the ship like she owned the place. I began to think that maybe she did. Only one way to find out, so I struck up a conversation with her.

"I couldn't help but notice that you seem quite familiar with the crew. Do you take this cruise a lot?' I asked.

"Yes,' she nodded, 'I've been on this cruise and many others in the last few years.'

"Wow,' I shook my head, 'we could barely afford this one.'

"Me too!' She agreed, 'but I found a way to do it!'

"You won the lottery, right?' I guessed.

"Nope, quite the opposite,' she grinned. 'I sold my house, my car and everything I had, and I just, well, live on cruise ships . . . just go from one to another.' She gave a little dismissive wave for emphasis. 'And I plan to keep doing it, indefinitely.'

"My mouth dropped open so wide, I am sure she could see my tonsils.

"You see," she whispered, conspiratorially, 'when you have no house you have no mortgage, or taxes, or insurance, or upkeep, which I was having to hire people to do because I could no longer do it myself. You don't have a car that needs insurance, gas and maintenance. You have no place to store your earthly treasures so why have them at all? You have no place to go home to, so the adventure never ends. It costs me less to cruise forever than my whole boring life did before I discovered this ingenious solution.'

" 'With passage on a cruise ship,' she went on, 'comes your private room, housekeeping service, all of your meals, shipboard entertainment, a medical staff, the list goes on! You are, literally, ENTITLED to everything you want and need, and it is at your fingertips 24-7.'

"What about your family?' I asked, incredulously.

"They love it! I put into ports-of-call where I can spend my shore time visiting with them instead of sight-seeing. Plus, now that my husband has passed on, my kids are relieved that they don't have to take care of me or try to make me happy.

"When they are able, they join me on a cruise. I tell you, my grandkids think 'Grandma's house' is *pretty cool.*" She drew the last two words out with a wink and a nod.

" 'Raise your hand,' I prompted the restless rascals before me, 'if your grandma's house has an aqua park and a movie theatre; how about a shopping mall and a food court?' The kids looked around at each other, but no hands went up.

"At that, the cruise ship grandma wished me Bon Voyage and went on her way. I watched her stop briefly to chat with a couple of ship chefs who greeted her with friendly smiles.

"As she continued down the corridor, the chefs drew curtains across the buffet table behind which they began to create their next tempting display of culinary choices. I collapsed into a comfy lounge chair nearby to pursue my pastime of people-watching which was, at that point, pretty boring because the area was nearly deserted.

"Eventually, my lazy gaze was drawn to a boring gentleman who casually arrived on the scene. There was nothing casual about his intent, however. As he passed the cordoned off buffet, he snaked a hand between the closed curtains and withdrew two bread rolls. Glancing about, he grabbed two more. Suddenly, he appeared to be overcome with a feeding frenzy, and began stuffing his pockets furiously with rolls. He dropped a couple on the floor in his haste. When he could hold no more, he looked around again to see if he had been detected, then waddled off as fast as his ill-gotten bounty would allow. My boredom gone in a flash, all I could think was 'What just happened here?'

"He didn't see me, but he also failed to notice that his naughty behavior was being taped by one of those pesky wall-mounted cameras, that continuously recorded all ship-board activity. You can imagine his dismay and humiliation when it was replayed for the amusement of the entire crowd of passengers at the final assembly."

My boys' shoulders all slumped, dejectedly.

"The thing that puzzled me most about his sneaky behavior was that if he had just presented his ID card an entire staff of waiters would have treated him like royalty. Since everything was a part of the cruise, our ID was the only thing needed to entitle us to all the food we desired.

"The Book warns us that '*deeds done in the darkness will eventually be exposed by the Light* (Luke 8:17, paraphrased),' so yes, he got what was coming to him. But, at the same time, don't you think it was kind of sad that he felt the need to steal?"

Just as my fascinating new cruise-dwelling acquaintance had pointed out, did he not realize that he was **entitled**? The ID card in his possession gave him access to everything he could possibly desire, just as the cross of Christ's salvation gives us access to the riches of God's kingdom.

In The Book, Peter's first letter praises God for the great inheritance that is ours through the resurrection of Jesus Christ. We are eternally ENTITLED as recognized children of the King of Kings!

Do not store up for yourselves treasures on earth, where moth and rust destroy, and where thieves break in and steal. (Matthew 6:19)

But all things become visible when they are exposed by the light, for everything that becomes visible is light. (Ephesians 5:13)

For nothing is concealed that will not become evident, nor anything hidden that will not be known and come to light. (Luke 8:17)

Blessed be the God and Father of our Lord Jesus Christ, who according to His great mercy has caused us to be born again to a living hope through the resurrection of Jesus Christ from the dead, to obtain an inheritance which is imperishable, undefiled, and will not fade away, reserved in heaven for you, (I Peter 1:3-4)

Chapter
EIGHTEEN

SOUVENIR SHOPPING

"My Pa had told me many stories of being stationed in Alaska during WWII and, later as missionaries, my aunt and uncle survived the 1964 Alaskan earthquake. Since then, I had longed to see Alaska for myself, so I was excited to realize my dream through the 5-stop Cruise I have been telling you about.

"Several weeks ago, I told you about the cruise director who gave us an overview of the week ahead. In addition to the unique charms of each port-of-call, we would have an opportunity to purchase souvenirs from local shops.

"Well, who doesn't like souvenirs, right?" The grins and nods on the faces in front of me were nearly as enthusiastic as the cruise director had been. "In fact, when I come home from a trip, what do you think are the first words I hear from my family?"

Before the circle of children could even raise their hands, the congregation thundered in unison "What did you bring me?" I finally had to hold up my cruise guide to get the happy high-fiving to wind down.

"She warned us to stay away from shops that were not listed in the ship's directory, as they might be disreputable. Then, just to make sure we heeded her advice, she announced loudly that she had just received coupon books, which, for $20, would entitle us to hundreds of dollars of free gems and jewelry at the various stops. Coupon books for souvenirs! Now she had me. I was hooked.

"At the first port of call, we rushed from shop to shop along the waterfront, collecting our free gems. At one shop I also bought an adorable heart-shaped acrylic pendant. As the shopkeeper rang up my purchase, I asked him where it was made. He told me the jewelry artist was located in Duvall, Washington (which he pronounced with a phony French flair). The little country town of Duvall is less than three miles from my home! I could have bought the same piece at a booth in my local Farmer's Market for a fraction of the price!

"Many shops had already run out of the coupon freebies, so we vowed to hurry a little faster at the next port. By the time we reached the third port, I was pretty tired of racing in and out of oddly similar shops with strikingly familiar merchandise and, frankly, I was bored. I stumbled into a shop that was not on the list but appeared to have some genuine local crafts. What a wonderful experience it turned out to be.

"I asked the proprietor why they were not listed in the cruise ship directory. She told me, somewhat bitterly, that the shops in the book sprang up each year during cruise ship season, and, just as quickly, disappeared when it was over.

"These fake shops were strategically placed along the waterfront enticing the cruise ship passengers to visit them and only them with the promise of practically worthless chips of gems. She said those same shops could be found at every cruise ship destination all over the world, but they certainly did not represent the local artisans, nor did they do anything for the local economy.

"I couldn't believe how easily I had fallen for the cruise director's convincing act. She had deceived me into wasting half of my trip. The coupon book was bigger than the baggy of trinkets I had wasted time collecting. I held the book and the baggy up together so the group could judge my stupidity for themselves. Even the youngest ones nodded sagely.

But do you know what made me feel even worse? **I had not seen Alaska!** You better believe I made up for it during the rest of the trip.

Where to start? I was weighing my options when a local bus rolled to a stop. The door opened, and the driver nodded at me. I didn't realize I was standing at a bus stop, but I took his friendly invitation as a positive sign, and I stepped aboard.

"Looking around, I realized I was the only tourist on board. As I rode the bus to the end of the line and then back, the locals took me under their wings, as it were, pointing out scenic and historic attractions along the way and regaling me with cultural stories. As they got off at various villages, they included me in their farewells and as new riders boarded, they introduced me to them.

"About an hour later, the bus returned to our port-of-call with all my new friends and me. As I neared the exit, the bus driver who had never said a word, gave me an approving nod and a smile as if to say, *Now, you have seen Alaska!*

"What about us? When have we missed the real Alaska for a sad imitation?

"How often are we distracted from the teachings of our Lord by misleading temptations. Satan's primary purpose in the Garden of Eden, as well as this world, is to mislead us with tempting but false and forbidden fruit.

"Guess what, young ladies," I said to quell any question among my listeners that a competition was still in progress, "I was, sheepishly, embarrassed to have been duped by a persuasive cruise director announcing 'good news' about valuable coupon books. Falling for her lie made me realize that I need to be just as wary of those who cause me to listen to false teaching or tempt me to stray from the way God wants me to go.

"So, boys, two gotchas. Girls, two gotchas. The score is tied. Game over!

"We will all be faced with traveling options as we go through life. As hokey as it may sound, the option we must hold out for is the one where Jesus, our Savior is sitting at the wheel. He is the only one who can guide us down the route His Father has prepared for us to follow.

"When I get off the bus of this world, I want to see my Savior's satisfactory nod as I exit. I want to have done what I needed to do on this earth; gone where I needed to go, met those I needed to meet, learned from those who had something to teach me, shared my "Good News" with those who needed to hear it, and feel the anticipation of new life in eternity.

"Your journey is different than mine, but the outcome is the same. Choose wisely."

Now I urge you, brothers and sisters, keep your eye on those who cause dissensions and hindrances contrary to the teaching which you learned, and turn away from them. For such people are slaves, not of our Lord Christ but of their own appetites; and by their smooth and flattering speech they deceive the hearts of the unsuspecting. (Romans 16:17-18)

When the pastor invited the congregation to pick a hymn, a little boy named Tripp asked for the classic "seventh inning stretch" favorite, and Sharon, our organist, didn't miss a beat playing it to the delight of the congregation. That fit right into my children's sermon.

"There is just something about balls," I said, passing around a ball carved from rock that I had unearthed. "This is one that young Native Americans who lived in tents tossed back and forth or batted with sticks." I handed it off and the children passed it in a circle.

"I brought some other balls for us to look at too," I announced as I dug into my basket and proceeded to distribute them:

"This first one is a member of the racquetball family and is called a **tennis ball.** It is very resilient, can take a good pounding, and still bounce back.

"It is not to be confused, however, with this one which is called a **croquet ball.** It can take a lot of hard knocks but keeps right on playing.

"Here is another one that is used to getting kicked around a lot. It is a member of the Rugby family and is called a **soccer ball.**

"Some people say it is a relative of this **football,** but it must be a very distant cousin." I shrugged. "As you can see, a football has a unique genetic shape. It also has an ingratiating way of insisting it's not about *them*, it is about the *team*." That one earned me a chuckle from one of the men, so I tossed it to him.

"Here is a happy-go-lucky guy, always whistling. It's called a **wiffle ball**. There's not much substance to it. In fact, it kind of absorbs whatever is around it.

"Then there's this **hacky sack**. It's a down and dirty street ball that's a real public servant because it is an alternative to boredom which, if left unattended, can often lead to mischief.

"A **basketball** may be full of hot air, but it can really draw a crowd. It nets a lot of attention in the gym, on the street, in a driveway, on a playground.

"Oh, I almost forgot another biggy." I dove behind the lectern and wrestled out a bowling ball bag. "I don't know how people play this game at all. I can't even lift it! A bowling ball is just plain full of itself. Besides, I think it is kind of snobbish to require a private bag!

"Here's another one that can be kind of annoying. It is called a **Magic Eight Ball**, it's a real know-it-all and has an opinion about everything.

"A lot of people just can't seem to get enough of this next one. Called a **golf ball**, it is very tightly wound and hard to manage, but it protects itself by being hard shelled.

"Oh, I bet you guys know this one—the **rubber ball**. It has lots of nicknames, super ball, space ball, beach ball, bouncy ball to name a few." I tossed it toward the wall where it ricocheted around the room for a while, with a couple of kids chasing after it. "As you can see, it is the life of the party, flitting here and there, always ready for a good time.

"Now, here is one I use a lot. It is called a **stress ball**. I don't have a clue what it has in it, but when I squeeze it, all my tension just melts away. Several moms in the room stuck out their palms to give it a go.

"Of course, we *must* have a **baseball** or a **softball**. It is a well-developed individual that is multi-layered and smooth-skinned. Lightly, I tossed one of them up in the air.

"Anybody in the mood for a round of tennis?" I asked. Kenny started to hand me the tennis ball he was holding but I waved it away.

"That's OK. I thought we would use this one." I held the baseball high but was emphatically informed by the group that we couldn't use the baseball to play tennis.

"Why can't we? It's small and round. Why won't it work just as well?"

Kiera cut through the din of explanations by raising her hand, so I called on her.

"Each ball is made for a game it's supposed to play. That's its purpose, and you have to have the right one or it doesn't work."

I smiled at her. "I couldn't have said it better myself. You deserve a prize! How about a **gumball**? It's a sweet, long-lasting ball that comes in different flavors. Yum!" All eyes were on the treat.

"That's how it is with us." I said as I passed one out to each of the children. "We are uniquely different. We each have a purpose and have been created to do something planned by our Creator." The children chomped on their gum in silence.

"Each of us needs to discover what that is. You see, the game of life isn't just about winning and losing, it is about discovering what God's game plan is and then having a ball out there. It makes you sing 'Take Me Out to the Ballgame' with a whole new meaning.

Sharon and the congregation started belting it out. I knew they would.

And we know that God causes all things to work together for good to those who love God, to those who are called according to His purpose. (Romans 8:28)

For it is God who is at work in you, both to desire and to work for His good pleasure. (Philippians 2:13)

Chapter
TWENTY

SEEK
HIS FACE

"*The Lion King* is a great show, right?" The kids all nodded vigorously. "I loved watching Simba grow up and practice being as brave as his father."

I clawed the air with both hands and sang, dramatically, "I la-ha-ha-augh in the face of danger!

"Baby Simba was sure a good singer." Their puzzled faces gave me the cue I needed.

"What, you don't remember that?" When they shook their heads in unison, I laughed and admitted, "Neither do I. I made that up. He did say it, but he didn't sing it.

"However, there is a kind of show called *opera* that sings everything! No words are spoken, everything is sung. Several times a year I get all dressed up and go with my husband and our friend Betty to the Seattle Opera.

"We just saw a two-act opera that made me have to really think about how God talks to us. At a crucial point in the story, Norma, a druid priestess, had a decision to make, so she retired to the temple to pray. When she emerged to address her Celtic congregation, a huge golden disk lowered slowly from the ceiling until it spanned the entire stage. She sang 'Quiet, the god speaks.' All eyes were riveted upward as they waited to hear the god answer her prayer.

" '*Now why can't God do that when we pray?*' I wondered as I sat there in that opera house. '*The answer to our prayers would be so much easier to understand if a visible divine entity audibly told us what to do in the presence of witnesses!'*

"Then I imagined God answering, 'Been there, done that, didn't work.' It occurred to me that, in the Garden of Eden, before Adam and Eve decided they wanted to do things their own way, they DID have the daily privilege of walking and talking with God. They could see Him, touch Him, and hear Him.

"Because Adam and Eve were made in the image of God, they shared a measure of His goodness. When they disobeyed Him and stopped being good, the glory of His goodness became toxic to them. Although it makes Him very sad, God denies Himself any physical contact with us for our protection.

"The only thing I can think of to compare it to is Superman's reaction to Kryptonite. When he lived on Krypton it had no effect on him, but out of his natural element, just a tiny bit of Kryptonite became deadly.

"Remember when God gave Moses the Ten Commandments?" A few hands shot up at the remembrance. "The Book says that Moses' face got so bright that the people could not bear to look at him and demanded that he cover himself with a veil when he was around them. Now I would have liked to have seen that! How about you?

"The point is," I said, shaking my head, "we sinful humans, apparently, cannot even tolerate being in the presence of someone who has *been* in the presence of God.

"As long as God stayed hidden in a cloud, Moses could have personal conversations with Him up close. But when he asked to see God's glory, God compromised by letting Moses see just His back.

"Then our heavenly Father put his brilliant plan to, once again, be able to walk and talk with us into action: He said, 'I will become like them.'

"Through Jesus, the Son of Man, God could, once again, interact with us physically without damage. He spent three years of quality time with us, audibly and visually answering the most important question we can ever ask ourselves, 'What must I do to be saved?'

"Well, what might *being saved* mean from a kid's point of view? What if you were really being disobedient in a store, and your mom says, 'Just wait until I get you home, then you'll be sorry!' What do you think she is going to do?

"Tell Dad?" they ventured, tentatively.

"Yep, she is going to tell your dad how you acted and just the thought of what punishment you might get from him is enough to make you think twice. Just so, each of us must eventually go home and stand face to face with our Father who is in heaven."

I put my hands on my hips for emphasis and said, "When we stand before Him and He says, 'Well? What have you got to say for yourself?' Guess how we get out of the punishment we deserve?"

I got a lump in my throat as I heard even the smallest ones in the group whisper, "Jesus saves us!"

After I cleared my throat, I went on. "Yes, Jesus steps between us and our heavenly Father and says, 'Dad, I already took the punishment for this one.'

"I still wish I could have immediate answers to my prayers like the fake god did in the opera but even when I ask for my earthly dad's help, sometimes he makes me wait.

"Though we don't see and touch and hear Him, we have our answer in The Book. If we believe in Jesus, one day we will see God in all His glory, face to face. And what a day that will be!"

So when Aaron and all the sons of Israel saw Moses, behold, the skin of his face shone, and they were afraid to approach him. (Exodus 34:30)

He further said, "You cannot see My face, for mankind shall not see Me and live!" (Exodus 33:20)

Then the LORD said, "Behold, there is a place by Me, and you shall stand there on the rock; and it will come about, while My glory is passing by, that I will put you in the cleft of the rock and cover you with My hand until I have passed by. Then I will take My hand away and you shall see My back, but My face shall not be seen." (Exodus 33:21-23)

Who, as He already existed in the form of God, did not consider equality with God something to be grasped, but emptied Himself by taking the form of a bond-servant and being born in the likeness of men. (Philippians 2:6, ESV)

For now we see in a mirror dimly, but then face to face. (1 Corinthians 13:12)

Chapter
TWENTY-ONE

WARNING
LABEL

The kids are always curious when I am lugging a bag of props so they all hurried toward me to see what was in my huge sack.

"I find it interesting that just about everything we buy comes with some kind of warning label," I began.

"Cigarette packets sternly advise that *the Surgeon General has determined that inhaling tobacco smoke can cause lung cancer.*" I held my nose at the smell as I drew an empty cigarette box from my bag.

"The labels on older children's pajamas might tell us that they are *not fire retardant.* Labels on newer versions warn us that the chemicals used to make them fire retardant *may be harmful to our health.*" I held up one of each as if I were weighing both consequences.

"Alcohol bottles caution us that its contents *should not be consumed by pregnant women.*" Pointing to a wine label, I added, "*and no drinking before you drive your car.*"

Next, I lifted out an assortment of cleaning products as I cautioned,

"*Do not inhale them.*"

"*Do not get them in your eyes.*"

"*Do not swallow them.*"

"And *do not combine them with other toxic products.* Whew!"

"Electrical appliances warn you *not to use them if you are immersed in water* and to *never work on them if they are still plugged in.* Duh!" I waved a hairdryer at them, menacingly.

"Okay— just one more." I plumped the object still hidden in my bag, and the kids were so intrigued by its size that they backed up a bit.

"My favorite is the warning on a huge, ugly, white tag attached to every cushion I have ever bought." I took my time wrestling a very large pillow from my sack and pointed to the dangling tag.

"It says *'DO NOT REMOVE UNDER PENALTY OF LAW!'* As a child, I used to wonder what horrible fate would befall me if I disobeyed. Never, in all my life, have I removed one!"

That earned an explosion of laughter and nods all over the room.

"Warnings are important and meant to be taken seriously." I set the bag down and reached into my purse. "I have another warning that you see every time you pay for something."

"Who can read these four words?" I asked pointing to the back of a dollar bill.

The kids leaned forward and one of the older boys shouted out, "IN GOD WE TRUST!"

"From the lowliest penny to the highest bill, each is stamped with that instruction. Why?" I asked. "Because it's not money that we should trust." I put the dollar back in my purse. "And wanting more and more money and things is a problem.

"The Book warns us not to give in to greed, but our nature is not just to **want**, but to **want more**. We have an urge not just to **have** but to **hoard.**

"Remember when Moses was leading the Hebrew people through the Wilderness? God told Moses to warn the people not to worry about being fed and promised to give them a fresh batch of manna every day. Well, some of them decided to save some *just in case.* Guess how God punished the ones who wouldn't trust in Him?"

From my expression of horror, my listeners anticipated the worst and they collectively shivered and gasped when I shrieked, "The manna had worms all over it!"

"Ewwww!" Their faces scrunched in disgust.

"When God finally gave them their own land, He told them every seventh year was to be a vacation—for EVERYTHING! That was the rule and the warning. Do you think they followed it?" The kids shook their heads, hesitatingly.

"Instead, they would take a break, but rent their land out for someone else to grow a crop on so they could still make money from it! That wasn't giving the land a vacation. Guess how God punished them for their greed?"

"Worms again!" several in the group objected, smacking their foreheads.

"No, it was *much* worse. He sent them back into captivity for seventy loooong years so the tired land could rest.

"The Book warns us that the love of *money is the root of all evil* so **In God We Trust** is one of the best instructional warning labels there is. If we would just pause and heed that warning as we count our cash, perhaps we would learn not to place our trust in something as unstable as money.

"One cent won't get you much these days," I said as I dropped a shiny penny into each of their hands, "so, just hang on to it and read its warning label once in a while. We have a loving God who has promised to provide for us, just like He did for the Israelites, if only we would trust in Him."

I set the pillow on my lap and pulled on the tag.

"I don't know what *really* happens to someone who cuts off that pillow tag that threatens *Penalty of Law if removed*; but I do know the punishment for snipping **In God We Trust** off our money. It is called 'defacing the currency'!"

At this point, I read quickly from an official-looking document: "It is a violation of Title 18, Section 33, of the United States Code which warns:

"Whoever mutilates, cuts, disfigures, perforates, unites, or cements together, or does any other thing to any bank bill, draft, note, or other evidence of debt issued by any national banking association, Federal Reserve Bank, or Federal Reserve System, with intent to render such item(s) unfit to be reissued, shall be fined not more than $100, or imprisoned not more than six months, or both.

"Who knew?" I shrugged and winked. "Apparently, God did!"

Moses said to them, "No one is to leave any of it until morning." *But they did not listen to Moses, and some left part of it until morning, and it bred worms and stank; and Moses was angry with them.* (Exodus 16:19-20)

...to fulfill the word of the LORD by the mouth of Jeremiah, until the land had enjoyed its Sabbaths. All the days of its desolation it kept the Sabbath until seventy years were complete. (2 Chronicles 36:21)

Beware, and be on your guard against every form of greed; for not even when one is affluent does his life consist of his possessions. (Luke 12:15)

For the love of money is a root of all sorts of evil, and some by longing for it have wandered away from the faith and pierced themselves with many griefs. (1 Timothy 6:10)

Chapter
TWENTY-TWO
A COAT
AND TWO
HATS

Through Compassion International, Mugeni Loyce came into our lives in 1999, when our church signed up to sponsor a child in Uganda. Pronounced "Lois," Loyce was a somewhat shy looking little girl whose birthday was listed as: "**1991, Exact date unknown.**" Her bio said there were seven children in the family and both parents were sometimes employed as farmers. Loyce's household chores were gardening, carrying water and washing clothes. Her favorite activities were hoop rolling and playing house.

She wrote to us regularly; at first through a translator and then, as her English improved, in her own handwriting. Over the years we could see her amazing faith in the Lord grow and mature through good times and bad; all of which she shared in her letters. There was always a Bible verse that had impressed itself on her tucked into the page. As she expounded on the verse and what it meant to her, it made me think of Jesus in the temple teaching the teachers.

In one heart-wrenching letter she wrote, "I put to mind that you are alive in the Lord's presence and the good work done over there (America). I am praying for God's protection upon your life and whatever work you do. Meanwhile, I would like to glorify God for His protection upon my life because when I had an HIV test, I was found negative, and for that, glory be to God." Though she lived in the middle of an AIDS epidemic, she prayed for our welfare first.

In another one she said, "Dear ones, this letter is accompanied with a photograph which I took with my friend, Sylvia, on Christmas day. We were ministering in the church with a song which goes: '*It was the given time when the Saviour came on earth. He came as a little baby in a lonely humble home...*' This song touched me, and I sang it joyfully. That is why you can see my mouth open and the hands swinging."

Our monthly support consisted of $28.00! That is correct—twenty-eight whole dollars. Her entire existence depended on that tiny check that would not even fill my gas tank.

Each year we were encouraged to send an extra $15 so the sponsored child could receive a Christmas gift. Compassion International took all the extra money and divided it equally among the children in the program. Thus, Loyce's actual gift might consist of somewhere between $11 and $14. At this writing, one U.S. dollar equaled 2085 Ugandan shillings.

Our favorite letter was always the one that arrived in January in which she would tell us how she spent her Christmas money. Two things were always at the top of her list: her tithe to the Lord, and 'school-going shoes.' Now, try to fathom that, after those two items, she STILL has money left over.

One year she told us her gift was 22,843 shillings of which she spent 8,000 shillings on her tithe and her shoes. Then, at first reading, it looked like she bought a coat for 10,000 shillings and two hats for 4,000 shillings. As I re-read it, however, I did a double-take. What she actually bought was a GOAT and two HENS; milk and eggs for her family.

By my calculations, after that, she still had 843 shillings left! Guess what she did with it? She took her WHOLE family to the sponsored Christmas dinner.

At this writing, it was hard for me to whine about the hard economic times we were supposedly going through, except for making sure we could still come up with $28 each month to send to her. If Loyce was not a living example of "the least of these" The Book tells us about, I don't know what would be!

At nineteen years of age, Loyce aspired to be a teacher. School had not been easy for her, and the stress of her advanced studies' entrance exams gave her unrelenting headaches and nosebleeds. She was not deterred, however. She said, "I will do my best on the tests, if we would please pray for her health." She also asked, politely, if we would consider continuing her support through the Leadership Development Programme.

Recently, I tacked her latest picture to my corkboard. This shy little girl is now a self-assured young woman with a strong conviction that God's hand is on her life, guiding her with loving purpose.

As you read this, look around the room that you are sitting in. Compare what you have to what she has.

Contrast her 'school-going flip flops' to your closet full of shoes—each pair designed for a specific purpose; school, church, snow, rain, plus a different style for each sport you enjoy.

Compare her 'hoop' to how many things in your life have 'wheels.' Even think about how many of those are still being paid for on credit.

How much time do you spend playing on digital devices while Loyce prepares herself for adult responsibilities?

Next time you turn on the faucet for a shower, picture a little girl carrying full sloshy buckets every day for the water needs of her family.

As you are separating your clothes into white and dark piles, picture Loyce carrying clothes to the community borehole and scrubbing them clean.

As you reach into the freezer for ice cream at the grocery store, pause to imagine her gardening in the hot sun. For that matter, weigh the cost of what you spend on groceries, fast food and dining out to what she lives on.

Oh, and by the way, I am pretty sure we can add care for the goat and hens to Loyce's daily responsibilities that were just listed.

Nope, our congregation of Christ-followers was not ready to cut her loose yet, no way, no how. She keeps us humble, her letters make us happy, and she continues to give us a wholesome perspective about what is really important—and, what is not!

Give that up for $28 a month? Not a chance!

And the King will answer and say to them, 'Truly I say to you, to the extent that you did it for one of the least of these brothers or sisters of Mine, you did it for Me.' (Matthew 25:40)

Chapter
TWENTY-THREE
PUTTIN'
ON THE
RITZ

"**I** have a little confession to make," I confided to the kids. My Sunday morning audience perked up, ready for something juicy. "I had to have braces on my teeth, just like some of you, only I had them at the same time my kids did."

"So?" Their expressions said. "What's the big deal?" They were clearly unimpressed, perhaps disappointed. But I had a plan.

"Okay, you kids who have had braces, what happens after you get them taken off?"

Their answers tumbled over each other,

"You can eat corn on the cob."

"You can brush your teeth better."

"You can chew bubble gum."

"Food doesn't get stuck in your teeth."

"You have to wear a retainer."

"Ah yes," I sighed, shaking my head. "You have to wear a retainer." I paused and then frowned. "If *your* mom is anything like I was with *my* kids, she probably told you to take good care of it and not to lose it, right?"

The moms all nodded and several of the kids had that deer-in-the-headlights look that told me they had suffered the consequences of not heeding her advice.

"Well, here is my confession." They visibly perked up for the details. "After I told my kids to take care of their retainers, wouldn't you know, I lost mine!" Now the group absolutely roared with delight.

"Oh, we eventually found it out in the grass on the front lawn, but it looked like the lawnmower had gone over it a few times. Boy, did my kids have a ball getting even with me." I surveyed my fellow moms and added as an aside, "How I got blessed with a house full of comedians is a question I am going to ask when I get to heaven, but this time, they outdid themselves." Both the grownup kids and the braces-wearing kids awaited the punchline.

"My kids said, 'Mom, we came up with a way to keep you from losing your retainer.' "

At that point, I took a suction cup hook out of my pocket, licked it, and stuck it to my forehead. From it hung my retainer, right between my eyes. The kids' eyes widened in horror, unsure whether they should laugh at me or not.

"They smacked this contraption on my face and assured me that, from now on, I would always know where my retainer was when I took it out of my mouth."

The kids pointed and laughed and discussed how this could possibly work. Since it looked like it was going to be a good long while before I could get the room to settle down, I started passing out an assortment of bright WWJD wristbands.

"What Would Jesus Do!" Several of the kids chorused before I could even ask what it stood for. One of them said, "I already have one."

"Really?" I asked, "What do you wear it for?"

"To remind myself when I have to make a decision."

"Does it work?"

"Sometimes," he admitted.

"Maybe you need *two* of them," I laughed, handing him another band, "one for each wrist."

Do you know that the WWJD idea is nothing new? Thousands of years ago The Book suggested doing that very thing. Moses told God's people a good way to remember His commandments was to *"Fix these words of mine in your hearts and minds; tie them as symbols on your hands and bind them on your foreheads"* (Deuteronomy 11:18, NIV). I touched the suction cup on my head for effect and then showed the kids a picture of a Jewish man with little leather boxes containing Scripture verses tied around his forehead, and his hand and arm.

"Those ancient words from God started a tradition of wearing our faith that has endured for centuries. Even today, some Jews still wear these little boxes. It might not be as common in America as it is in

Israel, but I do see lots of people wearing hats with faith symbols and sayings on them.

"Have you noticed that people don't just wear their faith on their foreheads and their hands? I see many of you wearing Christian T-shirts, including the pastor. How about jewelry?" I looked up at the congregation. "How many people are wearing a cross today?"

Nearly every hand went up, and we saw an assortment of necklaces, earrings, tie tacks, lapel pins, rings, and bracelets throughout the room.

"The problem is," I went on, 'No matter how hard you try, you can't make what is written on a piece of apparel travel from your clothes or your jewelry to your heart."

I crossed my arms over my chest for emphasis and shrugged, "All the Christian stuff we wear means nothing unless what they stand for gets deep down inside us where we can't lose them."

About that time, the suction cup on my forehead popped off.

"Like my retainer, AGAIN!" (don't tell me the Holy Spirit doesn't have perfect timing), I made a face. That just made them laugh harder.

"And now here's a riddle for you." I lowered my voice, mysteriously, "What has sixteen mouths and thirty-two eyes?" They looked at each other and shrugged collectively.

"Well, I am going to let you think about it this week and I will tell you the answer next time because," I said holding up a sign, "this episode is . . . **TO BE CONTINUED…**

You shall therefore take these words of mine to heart and to soul; and you shall tie them as a sign on your hand, and they shall be as frontlets on your forehead. (Deuteronomy 11:18)

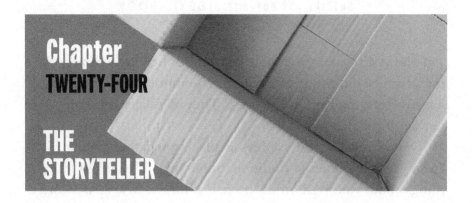

Chapter
TWENTY-FOUR

THE STORYTELLER

"Did anybody figure out the answer to the last riddle?" I dropped my voice, mysteriously, and repeated it for them. "What has sixteen mouths and thirty-two eyes?"

When I gently shook the box I was holding, several of them backed away, cautiously, concerned that whatever I had brought with me might try to get out by itself. I figured I better hurry. I opened the box and drew out a small clay figurine.

"In the Pueblo native American tradition, one of the oldest members of their tribe would be chosen as the Storyteller. The children would spend their days with that elder listening to the stories and learning the traditions of their culture."

The Pueblo Storyteller

BARBARA A. BABCOCK
GUY and DORIS MONTHAN

I showed the kids a Pueblo Storyteller figurine with its open mouth and a multitude of tiny listeners climbing all over it. "See, it has nineteen mouths and 38 eyes." They all relaxed and moved in to examine it closer.

"One of my favorite hobbies is piecing together family history, so I love this Pueblo tradition. Sometimes it's hard to find out things about your past unless there is someone to keep a record of your history and pass it on.

"At the ripe old age of 102, my great-uncle Laurence still loved passing on the historical family stories to the next generations. He relayed fascinating stories all the way from his Civil war grandparents to ancestors who came to America in the 1700's.

"But more importantly, Uncle Laurence was never shy about sharing his faith; what his Savior and Lord meant to him, and why. He loved to play piano and sing gospel hymns and, on his 103rd birthday, he sang in the church choir, as usual.

Mouths dropped open all over the room.

"The first time I looked at the Storyteller doll, I thought to myself that it looked kind of familiar. Then it came to me that it looks like familiar images of my favorite storyteller, Jesus, with children on His lap."

"The Book tells us that Jesus loved to have the children around Him." I held up another picture.

"You can see that the affection between them was pretty mutual as they practically crawled all over Him, nestling in His lap, hanging on His arms and sitting at His feet.

"Remember the verse we were looking at last week that said to *"fix God's words in your hearts and minds; tie them as symbols on your hands and bind them on your foreheads"* (Deuteronomy 11:18, NIV). I prompted them.

Several of the kids held up their arms so I could see they were still wearing their WWJD wristbands. Another one was wearing a T-shirt that read, *Please Be Patient. God Is Not Finished With Me Yet!*

"That passage in The Book about fixing God's words in your hearts and minds continues with *'Teach them to your children, talking about them when you sit at home and when you walk along the road, when you lie down and when you get up'* (Deuteronomy 11:19, NIV). That verse doesn't leave much out; when you are sitting, walking, sleeping, waking—pretty much means do it ALL THE TIME.

Knowing full well the answer to my question, I asked, "Does your Sunday School teacher give you Bible verses to memorize." I was rewarded with nods, and I called on one who raised her hand.

"We get to draw and color something to help us remember it while the teacher talks about it. Then she asks us next Sunday if we remember it. If we can, she puts a star on her chart on the wall.

"Can you say the one you learned today?"

"Not all of it," she said, "but my mom has the picture I drew, and I have all week to learn it."

I looked out over the congregation and, sure enough, her mom was holding up a pretty cool rendering of a girl walking on a path. She read the verse out loud, and it could not have been more perfect. Wow! God's timing is amazing!

"Make me know Your ways, LORD; Teach me Your paths" (Psalm 25:4).

"So, your Sunday School teacher gives you homework just like your school teacher does," I went on. "Then someone you love to be with every day helps you go over the lessons you learn in God's house. Your name on the teacher's chart gets a star but do you know what is even better?"

Candy, ice cream, and a host of other suggestions were proposed. I chuckled and went on.

"Nope! The most important thing you get when you know them by heart is that they are there when you need them to help you make decisions every day."

I turned to the child who was experimenting with WWJD bands on both wrists to help him remember to ask that question when he had a decision to make.

"Did that extra band help you last week?" I asked.

He shook his head "no," obviously not wanting to elaborate on it.

"You're not alone." I pulled up my sleeve and showed him that I was wearing five bands. "It didn't work for me either."

When the laughter died down, I went on. "There is only one way to make sure you really know what Jesus would do, and that is to make sure His words are deep down inside your heart where your mind and your conscience can remember it. The Book actually says that is where you need to keep it, in your heart.

Learn WWJD as if you were going to have to pass a quiz on it because, actually, you do! When your faith is tested by things that happen every day, your heart and mind will already be bursting at the seams with everything you need to know to pass with flying colors.

You shall also teach them to your sons, speaking of them when you sit in your house, when you walk along the road, when you lie down, and when you get up. (Deuteronomy 11:19)

I delight to do Your will, my God; Your Law is within my heart. (Psalm 40:8)

Chapter
TWENTY-FIVE

GONE FISHIN'

"Who rode in the *Pirates of the CaringBeing* float in the parade?" Every hand went up in my young group. No surprise, since it's one of our community's ministry highlights of the year.

Even Homer and Oscar, the star creations of our puppeteer Stephanie, were waving through portholes in the galleon, and 4-month-old Rowan in pirate garb smiled at the crowd from the arms of Captain Big-Hearted-Bill at the helm.

"This morning, I want to recall another float we entered in the parade a few years back. Something happened that day that illustrates a story you all know from The Book.

"A whale constructed of gray fabric was stretched over a PVC pipe skeleton and placed over a pickup with its mouth gaping wide over the windshield so the driver could see where he was going.

"A long fish tail hanging over the trailer hitch waved back and forth as if it was moving through the water." I moved my arms together in imitation. "All of the kids, including a baffled exchange student from Taiwan, sat in a wooden boat towed by the truck disguised as a whale as if they were pursuing the giant fish with fishing poles.

"Meanwhile, in the cab of the pickup, my son Chalon was manning a hand-cranked waterspout. Every time the parade came to a halt, he would crank like mad so that a geyser of water would emerge from the whale's blowhole and drench the crowd watching the parade and the kids in the boat." The kids smiled at the thought. "It was a hot July day, so the unexpected spray was actually refreshing.

"I met them at the end of the parade route and about had a heart attack when the truck driver and my son emerged from the cab. Their faces were almost purple, and they were so dehydrated they could barely stand up!"

" 'Mom! I didn't think I was going to make it! It was, like, over a hundred degrees in the cab of the truck, and the whale 'costume' kept any air from getting in at all. Then, I had to get up the energy to crank the water spout every time we stopped. I thought I was going to die!' "

"As Chalon threw himself out of the suffocating truck, I couldn't help but picture God's chosen fish vomiting Jonah up on a beach."

The Bible story of Jonah and the Whale never seems to lose its appeal, so the listening kids were immediately "hooked."

"If Chalon was in that bad of shape after about an hour inside the belly of our fake fish, can you just imagine what Jonah was like after three days and three nights inside the real thing?" I rocked back and forth to mimic his ride.

"I can't even fathom what was going on in Jonah's mind as digestive juices gurgled around him. *Okay, I have been eaten and it is so agonizing! I have been praying like mad, just let it be oveeeeer* !

"At the same time, this big fish is thinking, *Oh, I feel so sick. I have a horrible stomachache.*" I clutched my stomach and groaned, "*I feel like I am going to throw up and, then, MWAAWW!*" " The kids were rolling in the aisles and holding their sides, but I went on gamely.

"God had told Jonah firmly to go and tell Nineveh they were going to be destroyed if they didn't shape up." I practically yelled the instructions and then continued. "That would be like God telling you to go, all by yourself, and tell a gang of bullies at school that if they didn't shape up God was going to take them out!

"Jonah wasn't just like *I don't wanna!*" I whined, wringing my hands. "He actually ran away."

"In Psalm 139, The Book asks, 'Where can I go that You (God) are not there?' Sure enough, God pursued him with a huge storm that threatened to wreck the ship he ran away on. God allowed the ship's sailors to use their pagan fortune-telling custom to help them figure out what to do and guess who it pointed to? Jonah!

"Things were so bad by then that Jonah realized he was going to die either way. So, he told them, 'Yeah—it was me. Go ahead and throw me overboard.'

"They didn't want to and even asked Jonah's God to forgive them as they gave him the heave ho! Kerplop! In he went." I heaved my arms over the side of the railing.

"The minute they tossed him into the water, do you remember what happened?"

They all nodded, mesmerized by a familiar tale they never got tired of hearing.

"The storm stopped. Just like that. It was as if God were saying, *Yeah—it was Me. Go ahead and thank Me for it.* The pagan crew was so amazed that it worked, you better believe they worshiped Jo-nah's God!

"Scientists don't know the reason why sick and dying whales intentionally beach themselves. Jonah's whale may have deliber-ately stranded itself on shore as it heaved its stomach contents, but the location of the beach was picked by its Creator! Even so, Jonah still had a long walk ahead of him to get to the city itself and I can't imagine he felt up to trudging any distance after his ordeal; maybe he rented a camel. Either way, God was, obviously, giving him no choice.

"What do you think something that has been eaten looks like and smells like after three days soaked in gastric acid?" I wrinkled my nose and furrowed my brow. "Jonah may not have had a clue the effect he had on the wicked people of Nineveh as he finally staggered into town to deliver God's message, but it worked. They did an about-face.

"You know what Jonah's reaction was?"

The kids looked at me like they had never heard this part of the story before.

"He was so mad he was practically sputtering, 'They deserved destruction not forgiveness!!' That kind of sounds like what a pirate does. 'I don't care who I hurt as long as I gets me way. Argh!'

"Sometimes I feel that way too and God has had to remind me I am out of line just like he reminded Jonah. After all, none of us is worthy of redemption and yet, here we are at the foot of the cross, begging for it."

For the sake of a whole world full of wayward pirates, the only plank that got walked was the one Jesus carried on his shoulder as he walked to his crucifixion on Mt. Calvary.

I pointed to the cross on the altar, and bowed my head slowly as I breathed,

"Thank you Lord, for being a Caring Being who forgives us anyway."

Where can I go from Your Spirit or where can I flee from Your presence? (Psalm 139:7)

Chapter
TWENTY-SIX
OF LOCKS
AND
KEYS

I don't know when my fascination with locks and keys began, but there seems to be one constant: I am unable to throw away any lock or key. In fact, I have an old box full of random keys and a few padlocks. I will say that for over a half a century, the contents of that box have served me well.

I have rescued a pet from a locked house by finding a key in my box that fit it. On more than one occasion I have found an old key in the box that would fit a vehicle that had none. I bought an old filing cabinet at a surplus store and found a key in my box that would secure it. There is an assortment of skeleton keys and specialty keys in there that I could probably sell online, but I might need them someday.

Keys are not like snowflakes where no two of them are alike. Keys are based on a mathematical principle that says: the odds of the key in your hand being able to open something it doesn't go to are so small, it's worth the risk.

The padlocks, on the other hand, are old, durable, U.S. steel contraptions which intrigue me. They appear so pristine, so useful, *if I could just find a key!* I have been told that I could have keys made for them from a number stamped on the lock, but I have been over them with a magnifying glass and can find no numbers. On the other hand, maybe, I will one day find keys that will open them; so, in the box they stay.

My point is, someday I may find *something* that needs unlocking, and my box will hold the key that will do it.

Do you know that almost everyone has a box of keys in their house? Well, it isn't really a box, it is a book. **The Book!**

I have discovered that even people who profess no faith in God and go out of their way to deny or disprove His existence, still have a Bible somewhere in their home. They have never opened it and usually cannot remember where it came from: a family heirloom, a graduation or wedding gift, a hotel room. Yet, *something* keeps them from getting rid of it.

Maybe a beloved grandparent told them it was sacred. As such, they are prompted by superstition not to dispose of it. Or perhaps they keep it to argue more knowledgably with those who believe what is written in it. Nevertheless, there it stays.

I have so many Bibles in my home that it is hard to find room for them all. Why do I need so many? I couldn't bear to part with the one my grandma gave me. One is my mother's Bible that I carried at my wedding. Those aren't going anywhere! The Family Bible has priceless genealogy recorded in it. You get the picture? Then I have my Bible from college. It is in tatters and has so many notes written in the margins and so many verses underlined, you can barely see the original text. In fact, my daily Bible has to be replaced frequently for that reason.

I have discovered an interesting thing when I go back and thumb through one of my old ones. I cannot, for the life of me, remember why a passage I had underlined was so significant and things that are important to me now, went unnoticed back then.

Then I got it! They are *keys*. When you don't need what it opens, it is not important; but when you *do* need what it opens, you *really* need it and will search until you find the key that will unlock what is hidden. Each key in the Bible is there to open the eyes of your heart at exactly the right time.

The everyday events of life, be they good or bad, can be like frustrating little padlocks that need opening. The challenge is to find what or who holds the key that will do so. Never be reluctant to ask a friend or family member to cry or laugh with you. They just might hold the key to understanding what you are going through.

Christian companions are particularly good key carriers. In fact, as you get to know them, hear about their families, and learn what is going on in their lives, topics they write about to each other in personal letters would be easy for you to understand as well.

The same is true about the first Christ-followers, such as Paul, Peter, and Timothy, that you get to know by reading about them in The Book. As you come to be familiar with what is going on their lives, and hear about their relationships, even the letters between them, what The Book calls *epistles,* become like keys that can unlock something you are struggling to open in your own life.

A small treasure chest sat among the gifts at my son's wedding. It had ten tiny padlocks surrounding it, the keys to which were distributed among the guests. The bridal couple had to dance with everyone in the crowd asking for the keys until they found them all before the box could be opened. I thought it was incredibly clever and impossible not to get swept up in the game.

The Book, wherever it lies among the bric-a-brac of your life, just might be a treasure chest waiting for you to unlock and discover the marvelous things inside once the last catch to understanding it has fallen away.

There is an appointed time for everything. And there is a time for every matter under heaven. (Ecclesiastes 3:1)

I pray that the eyes of your heart may be enlightened, so that you will know what is the hope of His calling, what are the riches of the glory of His inheritance in the saints. (Ephesians 1:18)

NOTE TO READER: Ephesians is an example of an epistle. This verse was part of a letter Paul wrote to the saints in Ephesus.

And He will be the stability of your times, A wealth of salvation, wisdom, and knowledge. The fear of the LORD is his treasure. (Isaiah 33:6)

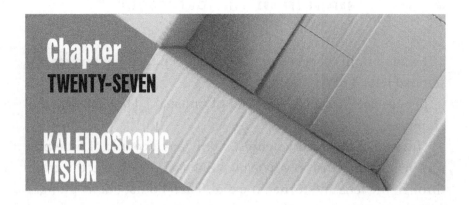

Chapter
TWENTY-SEVEN

KALEIDOSCOPIC VISION

"Did you know glass was first invented about three thousand years before Jesus was born?"

My weekly audience looked skeptical, as I began.

"Some sea merchants used a few hunks of the cargo they were carrying to sell to prop up their cooking pots over a fire on a beach. When the hunks melted and mixed with the sand and then cooled, it was glass! Can you imagine that?

"Not only did they have *glass*, they also took pieces of shiny metal to use as mirrors." My cherubs nodded, but their focus was on the curious bag I had nearby.

"In The Book, the apostle Paul told his listeners that we humans are only able to see spiritual things like they are reflections in a glass mirror." I held my hand up to my face as if looking at a mirror and corrected a wayward curl.

"They didn't make windows for their homes out of glass back then, but the people in the Corinthian church knew what it was." I wagged a finger, jokingly. They smiled, but their eyes were still diverted to the mysterious bag.

"I have something here I want each of you to try." As I opened my bag, they reached inside and reacted delightedly.

"Oh, I love these," one boy said while holding up a kaleidoscope. "So cool!"

I waited until everybody held one, then pulled out one for myself and held it up.

"These kaleidoscopes are kind of unusual." That got their full attention.

"Instead of tiny colored chips, it only has a couple of little mirrors inside it that distort what you point it at." I looked at the group through the lens and turned the dial. Then I burst out laughing.

"Not fair!" Several of them ventured, accusingly.

"Okay. I guess you deserve a try. All of you, point your kaleidoscopes right over here. Now close your eyes." I moved over into the spot and told them to open their eyes.

"Your face is funny looking!" They giggled.

"You're all mixed up!"

"Yeah, so I've been told," I said, wryly.

"OK, now let's try some other things," I went on. "Point it at the candle on the altar." All kids faced the same direction. "Now point it at the cross." We all shifted together. "Now one last one, I want you to point it at this open Bible I am holding up."

There was a lot of oohing and aahing as they turned the caps on their kaleidoscopes.

"Can you read it?" I asked.

"Not really, it is kind of confusing," was the general consensus.

"I think the people in the church Paul was visiting were confused too. I am sure they asked him, 'We are doing what you told us to do, what are we doing wrong?' " I waved my arms, dramatically, in frustration.

"He said you can speak in a language you don't know, like the disciples did at Pentecost; in fact, you can use all of the spiritual gifts the Holy Spirit gives you. You can give away your toys to children who don't have any. You can try, and try, and try, but it doesn't matter if you don't get the reason for it all.

"Paul wanted to make sure they absolutely understood what

was at the very top of God's list." I wonder if you know what that is? I asked as I covered The Book with a large white sheet. But before I could say what was written on it, my readers saw the answer.

"LOVE" they whispered, almost in awe.

When I removed the "love note," a few seconds later, something happened, so spontaneous and so unanimous, that it illustrated my point without a single word being spoken. Trying to make sense of something that isn't clear is very tiring. With one motion, they all put down their kaleidoscopes, obviously unwilling to spend any more time trying to decipher the page through it.

"As you can see," I said as they drew closer, "you were looking at that chapter we were just talking about through a bunch of tiny mirrors in your kaleidoscopes. It is a very famous passage, and I know everyone in this room is familiar with it.

"Paul told his listeners they were so busy doing so many other things they thought God would want them to do, that they forgot the most important thing: LOVE.

"So, Paul explained it very thoroughly for all generations. He made it very clear what LOVE IS: patient, kind, truthful, and never-ending."

I listed them on my fingers as I went, and their little fingers began to join me.

He described what LOVE IS NOT: envious, boastful, conceited, or selfish. It doesn't get its dander up, behave improperly or enjoy getting even.

"Finally, Paul itemized what LOVE DOES. Love bears, believes, hopes, and endures all things. He was pretty specific. I can't find a single detail he left out.

"Everything will become clear to us in heaven, but, for now, God wants us to practice, practice, practice, on the one clear thing that binds earth and eternity together." I drew my arms into a self-hug as I said the magic word, "Love." And the responsive whisper of the group was almost deafening in the sanctuary.

"LOVE."

If I speak with the tongues of mankind and of angels, but do not have love, I have become a noisy gong or a clanging cymbal. If I have the gift of prophecy and know all mysteries and all knowledge, and if I have all faith so as to remove mountains, but do not have love, I am nothing. And if I give away all my possessions to charity, and if I surrender my body so that I may glory, but do not have love, it does me no good.

Love is patient, love is kind, it is not jealous; love does not brag, it is not arrogant. It does not act disgracefully, it does not seek its own benefit; it is not provoked, does not keep an account of a wrong suffered, it does not rejoice in unrighteousness, but rejoices with the truth; it keeps every confidence, it believes all things, hopes all things, endures all things. (1 Corinthians 13:1-7)

For now we see in a mirror dimly, but then face to face; now I know in part, but then I will know fully, just as I also have been fully known. But now faith, hope, and love remain, these three; but the greatest of these is love. (1 Corinthians 13:12-13)

Chapter
TWENTY-EIGHT

JOGGING FOR JESUS

"Do you know what I saw this morning on my way to church?" I shouted from outside the sanctuary. "Lots of joggers! Considering how hard it is raining today, aren't you glad you are in here where it is warm and dry, getting some spiritual exercise instead?

"Our pastor's sermons come up with some pretty good tips to help us resist the things that cause us to get spiritually flabby. I know, I for one, have had a pretty rough week and have gotten kind of pudgy."

With that, I squeezed myself through the door frame and into the sanctuary. I had picked up a stretchy one-piece jumpsuit at a thrift store and stuffed the inside of it with balloons, so full that I had to cram my extra bulk through the doorway in waves. The next trick was going to be making it up the center aisle without wiping out a parishioner or two.

"Uh," I panted, "I think maybe you ought to stay in your seats this morning. I don't want to hurt anybody." Though the kids didn't look like they were too anxious to join me, they slowly trickled to the front of the sanctuary.

"This is kind of embarrassing, but today I got so mad at the driver of a car that almost ran me off the road, I wanted to do something to hurt him. The Book says that if we get angry with someone, it is the same thing as **murdering** them in our heart. But if we ask God to forgive us for feeling that way, He takes it away." I took a hatpin and popped one of the balloons. Everybody jumped, but the kids sat up a little straighter to get a better view.

"What about you? Did anybody take more than their fair share of something this week; maybe more treats than you were supposed to have?" I saw a few moms raise eyebrows at their children until a couple of hands went up, reluctantly. "That is called **greed,** and, if we are sorry, God can take that away too." I popped another balloon.

Then I leaned over and whispered to one little offender, "Were you sneaky about it?" The little head nodded. "That is called **deceit,** and Mom is not the only one who knows you did it. Even when you think you won't get caught. God sees it too. Did Mom forgive you?"

This time Mom and daughter both nodded.

"God forgives you too," and I popped another balloon.

"**Disobeying your parents** is big on God's list, so it is a good one to get rid of, don't you think?" I let the child closest to me stick the pin in a prominent balloon. "Ouch!" I whimpered, then chuckled. "Just kidding" and smiled at the child holding the pin.

"Does anybody in here have that new computer game I keep seeing on TV?" A couple of hands shot up, proudly. "I know somebody who works at the store, and he got me one before they even put them on the shelves," said one of the older boys, practically dancing in his seat. "Hmmm, that sounds like **boasting**, and if you want me to pop that balloon what do you need to do?"

"Oops, *sorry*," he said with a sheepish grin. I retrieved my pin and popped another balloon.

"Does anybody else wish they had that computer game?" Several of the others waved to me (including a couple of the dads). "Would you believe The Book calls that **envy**, and God doesn't like what it does to us." I popped another balloon.

"How did you all do this week?" I leaned to the collection of kids to my left. "Did anybody talk about somebody behind their back; maybe even hurt a friend's feelings?" I knew I had hit a nerve when a couple of them avoided my gaze.

"That is called **gossip**, and when you **slander** somebody's reputation, it creates **strife** that is hard to stop once it starts." Popping three balloons in quick succession made them all plug their ears.

"Friends are a good thing to have, so be careful how you treat others because **malice** is an **evil** thing that hurts you as much as it hurts them," I said as I popped two more balloons. "Besides, look how much better I am beginning to look without all that baggage."

By the time I got up to the steps before the altar, I only had one balloon left. "Did anybody stay in good spiritual shape this week? Are you proud of yourself because you didn't really sin too bad?"

Maybe the kids wouldn't have fallen for it if I hadn't raised my own hand, but several other hands went up, around the room.

"Sorry," I announced, "but that is called **arrogance** and, I don't know about you, but I don't want it in my life." I popped the last balloon.

"You see, when we look good on the inside it makes us look pretty good on the outside." I dug a wide cinchy belt out of my pocket and tightened it around my newly thinned waistline. "All of those people out there trying to get fit jogging in the rain are missing the point. I'm not saying we don't need physical exercise, but not at the expense of our spiritual exercise. That physical body is going to die someday, no matter how well we take care of it.

"The Book tells us to *'put off our old selves,'* in other words, get rid of all those bad things we just talked about." The kids suddenly plugged their ears in anticipation, then slowly took their hands away when they remembered I had nothing more to pop.

"Jesus died on the cross as a sacrifice for the sins of our old selves. Then The Book tells us when our renewed selves worship

God by offering Him our forgiven bodies as living sacrifices, He is pleased. Jesus died for us so we could live for Him. See how that works out?" Their nodding heads let me know they got it.

"Worship is exercise that takes care of the body in which you are going to live *forever,* so, it's important to stay in good spiritual health.

"One of the smallest entries in The Book begins with a verse that would also be a good one to say to those you love each morning. *Beloved, I pray that all may go well with you and that you may be in **good health**, as it goes well with your soul.* What a great way to start the day!"

About that time, it began raining so hard, that everyone looked toward the ceiling, and I just had to take advantage of the Holy Spirit's zinger.

"It makes me shiver for those poor souls out there catching a cold when they could be in here soaking up the Son." The worship team drummer was the first to get the Son/sun pun and punctuated it with a rim shot.

You are to rid yourselves of the old self, which is being corrupted in accordance with the lusts of deceit, and that you are to be renewed in the spirit of your minds. (Ephesians 4:22-23)

Therefore I urge you, brothers and sisters, by the mercies of God, to present your bodies as a living and holy sacrifice, acceptable to God, which is your spiritual service of worship. (Romans 12:1)

Beloved, I pray that in all respects you may prosper and be in good health, just as your soul prospers. (3 John 2)

Chapter
TWENTY-NINE

RACE RAP

"I'll bet you didn't know that I used to be a rapper," I told my fidgeting young listeners, "and I must have been a pretty good one because my "hit rap song" was requested over and over. It might have had a fairly small following—well, actually only one or two ever heard it performed—but it got rave reviews." Though I now had their attention, scrunched faces meant disbelief.

"Now before you go picturing me in the spotlight before a mic, with my cap on backward, together with slouchy, trendy clothes and iconic hand gestures, let me set you straight. My rap song was always done with my hands wrapped tightly around my steering wheel, and a couple of sweaty junior high football players in the backseat.

"You see, I wrote this little ditty for my son, who would suffer a case of nerves before every game. The closer my football mom station wagon got to our destination, the more agitated my little boy in his gangly man body would become. Finally, he would blurt out, 'Mom, could you do the song?'

I would set a cadence with my fingers on the steering wheel and then start rapping out the lyrics.

There's a clock that's tickin' and a foe that's kickin' up dust as he runs with you.

Don't let 'em say you tried, but you lost your stride, as the finish line came in view.

For the rest is sweeter at Jesus' feet than it is in the dust of the track.

So, keep your eyes on the line, you'll do just fine, as long as you don't look back.

A prize fighter falls in the rink, and he calls out in pain for the final bell.

He staggers to his feet, but the will to compete still lies on the floor where he fell.

The crowd cheers him on, and he fights 'til he's won, and the referee lifts his hand.

But he knows the real honor waits in the corner where the one that he fights for stands.

There's no sense livin' like you've been forgiven if you turn down the prize at the end.

When the game gets tough, and the fight gets rough, you gotta pray for a second wind.

St. Paul had a knack for not looking back, and he taught us to do the same.

Whatever your role, press on toward the goal, and let LOVE be your highest aim.

If you didn't want to cross the finish line, why'd you bother to run in the race?

Did you train so long and work so hard just to fall flat on your face?

Only you can choose where your place will be in the Winner's Circle of Eternity.

But I'll tell you what - if it was up to me

I'd pick myself up, set my eyes on the prize

And hustle back into the race.

By the time I got to the end, my routine was joined by a chorus from the backseat of "hustle, hustle, I said hustle—yeah, hustle back into the race" and the jitters had magically disappeared.

My 'Race Rap' was based on what Paul said in The Book in his letter to Timothy. Maybe Paul had been an athlete in his early years because he used the analogy of running a race over and over as he encouraged the early Christian churches in his letters. Are we really so different today?

"Why do thousands of fans flock to sporting events to yell and scream their support? They even do it from their armchairs while watching a game on TV, as if the players can actually hear them!"

The kids were looking around like they were unsure whether I thought that was okay or not, but that was not my point. I prayed that my conclusion would speak to all ages in the room.

"Why, on the other hand, are some of these same fans so hesitant to express themselves in church?" Puzzled looks turned into sheepish nods as I flashed two pictures on the screen behind me. One was a sparsely attended worship service. Some attendees had their noses buried in hymnals with lips barely moving, and others stood immobile, mouths firmly shut, simply enduring the experience.

The other picture was game-filled bleachers of the favorite local team with people, young and old, faces painted in team colors, flags and fists waving, mouths open, screaming so loudly their veins were standing out.

The traditional liturgy of my childhood concludes with the "Gloria," a hymn of praise that enumerates the accomplishments of the God we serve. Its words both convey our kudos for the great things He has done and encourage us as to acknowledge we're part of the winning team. *This is the feast of victory for our God.*

But if you looked around the room, you sure wouldn't know it. The way some of the worshipers mumble that cry of victory, you would think we were forcing down the leftovers of defeat. The Book says our worship is not acceptable to God unless it is genuine. He wants us to be genuinely involved, not genuinely bored.

I have heard it said, "We need to be Sunday people in a Monday world." In other words, let the world see the faith you profess on Sunday during the rest of the week. I agree, but I would amend that a little.

"I suggest we need to make sure we are *Saturday* people in a *Sunday* service. In other words, bring the same enthusiasm and passion for your favorite sports team when you worship and praise the One who holds your life in His hands.

"Now get out there," I coached, "and *hustle* back into the race!"

I have fought the good fight, I have finished the course, I have kept the faith. (2 Timothy 4:7)

...this people approaches Me with their words and honors Me with their lips, but their heart is far away from Me, and their reverence for Me consists of the commandment of men that is taught. (Isaiah 29:13)

God is spirit, and those who worship Him must worship in spirit and truth. (John 4:24)

Chapter
THIRTY

GOD'S
GREEN THUMB

I pulled a big juicy apple out of my sack and took a bite as I beckoned the children forward.

"Yum, this is so good! I just can't stop!" Actually, with my mouth full it came out more like "Yo mith tso goo, I juice can stoop."

As they circled around me, I swallowed, licked my fingers with just a little pop at the end of each one, and wiped my mouth with the back of my hand.

"Just picked these in my orchard this morning" I smacked, waving the apple with a bite out of it enticingly in front of them. "There were soooo many, I will have to go back tomorrow and finish. I look forward to lots of fruit to harvest from the trees in my orchard and they're really meeting my expectations, and then some." I set the apple core aside with a smile.

"If the crop turns out to be so-so," I said with a left-right twist of my wrist, "I can really identify with the story that Jesus told in The Book." I paused as they leaned forward, ready for a true tale. "There was a vineyard owner who ordered his caretaker to cut down one of the trees because it had not had any figs on it for years! The wise caretaker asked for permission to dig around it and fertilize it to see if he could get it to start producing fruit.

"Now, who can tell me what fertilizer is?" I heard a few gasps from the parents and the children were clearly embarrassed.

A couple of generations back, the subject of manure required using words they were forbidden to say at home, much less in church.

"OK," I sighed, "there is no delicate way to talk about animal excrement, so I am just going to call it 'doo doo.' Would that be alright?"

There was a smattering of giggles and a few raised eyebrows; everyone wondering how far I was going to stray outside the box this time.

"God is very specific about wanting to see spiritual fruit in our lives, and when He hasn't seen any for a long time, He will take action, just as the owner of the vineyard did.

"Sometimes," I went on, "the drastic steps God takes means uprooting us a little from our comfort zone. He does not tolerate spiritual laziness and has to shake our world a bit to bring us out of our laziness. If that doesn't work, He might have to dump on the, uh, *doo doo* to really get us back on track!" A few parents shook their heads, hiding smiles.

"That really stinks, huh?" It took a second for the play on words to sink in, so I let it hang in the air until you really could almost smell it.

"The Book tells us that sometimes, even letting us suffer problems and trials is part of God's efforts to get us to start producing fruit for His glory. When everything in your life is easy, after a while, it can feel like you are doing just fine on your own. When you begin to take credit for all the good things you have and forget where your blessings come from, you are stealing God's glory!

"If things get a little tougher and you realize there is nothing you can do about it, guess what eventually happens?" I slid to my knees and put my palms together.

"You pray!" They chorused.

"That's right, and I bet you do too! God loves seeing us get our knees dirty while we come crawling back to Him because He knows that the kind of fruit He wants to see in our lives will be sure to follow."

I opened my sack and invited the kids to take some apples for themselves.

"Oh, take more than just one. Take some for your parents too. There are plenty to go around." The kids dove in for this edible object lesson. "In fact, I will leave them on the table by the treats after worship. Take some to your neighbors. Take them for your lunchbox next week. Take as many as you want! That is what they are for!

"Just so, the spiritual fruit that God expects to see in our lives is to be so abundant that we can't possibly use it all. We just HAVE TO SHARE IT!" A few kids grabbed extra at that enticement.

"So next time you find yourself in deep *doo doo*, stop and ask if it was something you stepped in, or if it is something the Master Gardener is using to coax you into producing an abundant harvest of His kind of fruit to savor and to share."

And He began telling this parable: "A man had a fig tree which had been planted in his vineyard; and he came looking for fruit on it and did not find any. And he said to the vineyard-keeper, 'Look! For three years I have come looking for fruit on this fig tree without finding any. Cut it down! Why does it even use up the ground?' But he answered and said to him, 'Sir, leave it alone for this year too, until I dig around it and put in fertilizer; and if it bears fruit next year, fine; but if not, cut it down. (Luke 13:6-9)

We also celebrate in our tribulations, knowing that tribulation brings about perseverance; and perseverance, proven character; and proven character, hope; and hope does not disappoint, because the love of God has been poured out within our hearts through the Holy Spirit who was given to us. (Romans 5:3-5)

Chapter
THIRTY-ONE

THE WINDMILL

Just over the German border from Amsterdam, perched on the only hill for miles around is a little village called Kleve which we visited when our son married a local girl.

Our lodging was an old castle, and our days were spent sight-seeing and exploring. One of the highlights of the stay was a visit to a genuine working windmill, which the bride's father had an interest in.

The miller greeted us in broken English and took us to a long trestle table where he had mixed some of his grain flour into a fragrant dough. Dividing it into equal portions, he instructed us to knead and shape it into anything we wanted. When our creations had all been scooped into his wood stove, he said, "Now, I will take you on a tour."

I have always regarded windmills strictly in the pastoral sense. A watercolor painting of a dozen windmills on a flat green plain with clouds scudding across a blue sky, looks so peaceful. You can almost see the sails turning lazily, and you wish you were actually there. Well, now we were there, and it was NOT what I was expecting.

The inside of a windmill is anything but pastoral. It is an engineering marvel of hewn wood and forged metal, and we were standing in the middle of it. Just looking at diagrams in a computer search does not do justice to the sense of awe you get as you watch the mechanisms turn, and mesh, and work together.

In the center of the floor is a huge round timber called the 'King's Tree.' My new daughter-in-law admitted that it was pretty much impossible to cling to this *Koenigsbaum* when it was turning so quickly, but as they were growing up, she and her younger brother never quit trying.

Around the perimeter of the ceiling were the cogs that made it spin when the wind set the sails whirling outside the mill. At the base of this trunk was the bin where the grain was ground by the millstone when the windmill was in motion.

When the wind stops, so does the windmill. This is where the expression *"grind to a halt"* comes from.

The miller has no choice at that point, but to scoop up some of the grain in the bin and rub it between his thumb and finger to see if it is fine enough to be removed, or if it will have to remain in the bin until another wind comes up. This is *"the rule of thumb,"* a phrase commonly used even today to define an acceptable standard.

Our guide then took us outside to show us how the windmill captures the wind. Attached to the floating cap of the windmill is a fantail that responds to the slightest breeze. This cap is so finely balanced, that the fantail can rotate the heavy piece to which the sails are suspended to the perfect position to catch the wind.

Slowly, the sails begin to pick up speed, activating the marvelous mechanism inside the mill, turning the grain into the flour I had been buying so casually at the grocery store for years, without giving the process a single thought.

Then I blurted out that stupid tourist question that you immediately wish you could take back. "Is there a way to make it turn when there is no wind?"

The miller gave me a look that led me to believe that it was not the first time he had heard that question but still, derived a sense of amusement from the silly inquiry.

"No," he said shaking his head and pointing skyward for emphasis, "there are some things only God can do."

We can build an intricate windmill, but the power necessary to grind grain or even make electricity is still dependent on the great Creator of all that is.

When a hurricane devastates expensive upscale mansions built in a hurricane zone, insurance claims may or may not cover what is called an "Act of God."

Years ago, my husband I and our motorhome were picked up by a tornado and deposited five lanes away; shaken but, incredibly, unhurt. Believe me, a swirling funnel of wind is nothing to take lightly!

The Book says, *"Just as you do not know the path of the wind, and how bones are formed in the womb of the pregnant woman, so you do not know the activity of God who makes everything"* (Ecclesiastes 11:5).

It also tells us that God *"brings out the **wind** from his storehouses,"* (Psalm 135:7, NIV) and that *"no one has power over the **wind** to contain it"* (Ecclesiastes 8:8, NIV).

It took that wise little miller in Germany less than ten words to put into perspective what The Book has tried to tell us from its very first verse: **There are some things only God can do!**

Who has ascended into heaven and descended? Who has gathered the wind in His fists? Who has wrapped the waters in His garment? Who has established all the ends of the earth? What is His name or His Son's name? Surely you know! (Proverbs 30:4)

BELOW THE SAILS OF ALTE MÜHLE DONSBRÜGGEN IS INSCRIBED:
"IN STURM UND WETTER IS GOTT MEIN RETTER - 1824"
TRANSLATION: "IN STORM AND WEATHER, GOD IS MY SAVIOR"

Chapter
THIRTY-TWO

THEO
LOGICAL

I waited until the kids were all gathered around me before I asked for the sanctuary lights to be turned off. As the room was plunged into twilight, I could sense several of them inch a little closer to me, so I got right to it.

"The Book says, '*God is Light...*' I flipped on a three million candle power flashlight and aimed it at the wall of the sanctuary.

"The Book also calls Jesus '*the Light of the World.*' I took aim at the same spot and turned on a portable spotlight.

"At Pentecost, the Holy Spirit appeared among the disciples as '*tongues of fire,*' which is also light." I clicked on a sunlamp that had been strategically placed to glow on the same spot as the other two.

The kids and I looked at the wall together for a few minutes. I asked if anyone wanted to go up and separate the lights for me. Even the ones who usually raised their hands for everything did not jump at the chance.

"No takers? How come?" Several of them ventured to explain.

"I can't see the difference."

"The lines are blurry."

"It's all one big light."

I laughed, approvingly. "Bravo!" I said. "You got it!"

"Got what?" All the heads swiveled in my direction.

"You just described the Trinity," I explained. "You see, the word 'Trinity' is not in The Book. The dictionary definition is 'something made up of three parts.' " I held up three fingers.

"But The Book *does* describe God as three distinct *persons*." Then I held my right palm up before me in the classic benediction position as I asked, "What does the pastor say every week as the service is ending?" I gave them a clue by hinting with, "In the name of..."

"The Father, the Son, and the Holy Spirit," the kids finished for me.

"Why does the pastor do that? Why doesn't he just say, 'In the name of God?' "

They all looked at me, expectantly, so I went on. "Well, in the very first chapter of The Book, God is either plural, or He is, apparently, talking to Himself. He says, '*Let US make mankind in OUR image, according to OUR likeness.*' " I smiled and paused.

"Verse one of the Book says that '*the Spirit of God was hovering over the waters.*' John's gospel, calls Jesus '*The Word,*' and then John says that He was not only '*WITH God in the beginning, but that He WAS God.*' (John 1:1, paraphrased)

"It must have been important to Jesus to recognize all three lights as God, because His very last words to His disciples were to '*go, make disciples and baptize in the name of the Father, the Son and the Holy Spirit.*' " (Matthew 28:19, paraphrased)

At this point, even the adults were listening intently, so I stretched out my arms to include them as I went on, "Here, let me illustrate.

"If we don't acknowledge God as our Father, then there is no original Source who cares what happens to us." My tone had saddened. "If that's the case then everybody can do whatever they want, no matter how cruel or violent, because there is no such thing as sin." I flipped off the flashlight.

"If there is no *sin*, then we don't need somebody to save us from it, so there is no reason to acknowledge God, the Savior." I flipped off the spotlight.

"If Jesus did not *save* us, then there is no need for Him to leave us a source of power to be able to spread the word, so there is no reason to acknowledge God, the Holy Spirit." I flipped off the sunlamp.

The overhead lights in the sanctuary came back as I summarized, "See how it all fits together?

"Three separate lights were shining on the wall. Even though each one is a different source, together they become ONE bright light. It is hard to tell where one light ends and the other begins. I do not claim to be a theologian, but I do see some logic in simply visualizing that God-light as...the Trinity."

...God is Light; in Him there is no darkness at all. (1 John 1:5)

Then Jesus again spoke to them, saying, "I am the Light of the world; the one who follows Me will not walk in the darkness, but will have the Light of life." (John 8:12)

And tongues that looked like fire appeared to them, distributing themselves, and a tongue rested on each one of them. (Acts 2:3)

Then God said, "Let Us make mankind in Our image, according to Our likeness." (Genesis 1:26)

And the earth was a formless and desolate emptiness, and darkness was over the surface of the deep, and the Spirit of God was hovering over the surface of the waters. (Genesis 1:2)

In the beginning was the Word, and the Word was with God, and the Word was God. (John 1:1)

Go, therefore, and make disciples of all the nations, baptizing them in the name of the Father and the Son and the Holy Spirit. (Matthew 28:19)

Chapter
THIRTY-THREE

EL LUMINATION

"Remember last week when we used three different light sources to describe the Trinity?" My kids, as well as the grownups, nodded in recollection of the flashlight, sunlamp, and spotlight I had used on the wall of our church.

"Guess what? It's baaaack." It was obvious they couldn't wait to see what was next as they ran toward me.

The gang had been totally engaged in the previous illustration of a Triune God: A God who was not a bunch of gods like the pagans believe in, but ONE God that was three parts all rolled into one.

I wanted them to understand that each of God's sources of LIGHT has a specific purpose for us as we grope through the darkness of this world. But, eventually, there will be no need for their lights to separate.

"I want to try another experiment this morning, but first, everybody who knows how to read needs to have The Book in their hands." I held mine up as several of the kids scurried away to grab Bibles from various racks in the room.

Then I had an assistant back by the master light panel turn off the overhead lights in the sanctuary just as had been done in our last session. When the room had settled into a dim twilight I said, "This is about how much light there is in a theatre when you are trying to find your seat. Now I want everybody to open The Book to the twenty-first chapter of Revelation."

Everyone tried gamely but got no further than the title page. I turned the sunlamp representing the Holy Spirit back on. "Now can you find it?"

I heard pages turning wildly all over the room. Finally, someone said, "I can see the chapter heading at the top of the page."

"OK, we are making progress then. Can you read the verses yet?" There were a lot of negative head shakes.

I frowned in mock frustration and joined in with a negative head shake of my own.

"Well, unfortunately, the God-light of the Holy Spirit is all we have to go by until Jesus returns, so I guess we are going to need the sanctuary lights after all."

When they had come back on, I let the kids and the congregation resume their task of locating my chosen chapter in Revelation as I said, "When Jesus returns, His light will shine for us again." I turned the spotlight back on.

"Even better, in the new heaven and the new earth, the glory of God will shine forever." I turned the bright flashlight back on.

"That did the trick. Now I can read the words," someone confirmed.

"Really," I said as I furtively motioned to my sidekick at the back wall. He began slowly dimming the sanctuary lights until they were completely off. "Would you mind reading Revelation 21, verse 23 for us?"

He began reading, *"And the city has no need of the sun or of the moon to shine on it, for the glory of God has illuminated it, and its lamp is the Lamb."*

I let that sink in for a second, and then I said, "Did anybody happen to notice that the sanctuary lights were turned off again?"

The kids' mouths dropped open as they all looked up. Point taken. We didn't need the light of the world when we have the

Light of our Son.

"No Way! It's as bright as day!" I watched their incredulous expressions turn to elated high fives as they celebrated the outcome of our experiment.

"Yes," I beamed back at them, "and that is just this one room." As I said it, I realized the rest of the room was not joining our accolades.

The hushed congregation was a blur of heads bent over their Bibles. I recognized what they were doing because I know myself how hard it is to put The Book down after reading that verse. Whenever the darkness of the world is getting me down, I turn, *specifically*, to that chapter. By the time I get to the end of its description of the New Heaven and the New Earth, I can feel my heavy spirit lift in anticipation!

An anointed moment is not to be rushed so I let the kids take their time getting to their feet while I just stood there watching. As the adult faces slowly began to lift, I stage-whispered an obvious question they were probably already thinking:

"Can you just imagine what it will be like in our eternal home when the God-light is ALL the light we will ever need?"

As the kids and I began to rejoin the congregation, someone cleared their throat and reminded me that I had forgotten to turn the three lights back off.

"No," I smiled, "I didn't forget."

For the fountain of life is with You; In Your light we see light. (Psalm 36:9)

This is the message we have heard from Him and announce to you, that God is Light, and in Him there is no darkness at all. (1 John 1:5)

And the city has no need of the sun or of the moon to shine on it, for the glory of God has illuminated it, and its lamp is the Lamb. (Revelation 21:23)

Chapter
THIRTY-FOUR

ART FOR
SHORT

Recently, a snowboard accident had one of the older boys hobbling around on crutches, trying to soak up sympathy and still appear macho at the same time. He had assured us it was "no big deal" but just happened to have a sharpie on him so he could get as many signatures on his cast as possible. When I signed his cast, today's topic had popped into my mind.

"My doctor cautioned me for years not to be too hasty about having my bad knee replaced," I shared. 'It doesn't last forever. You are still too young for a replacement,' he would admonish.

"What do you mean they don't last forever? They are titanium after all, one of the hardest substances known to man,' I argued.

" 'Well,' he said, 'the material they use for the gasket in the new knee eventually wears out just like your old one did.'

"He talked me out of it as long as he could, but, eventually, an extra hard summer of farm work made a new joint necessary.

"In his office, the surgeon showed me a pristine model of a knee. 'This is an Articulating Trabicular Prosthesis' he told me, pointing to the shiny metal contraption he would insert in my leg bones.

A couple of the kids tried to repeat the tongue-twister and collapsed into giggles instead.

I pointed the sharpie I was still holding at one of the boys and asked the gang why we called him Eddie instead of his real name, Eduardo, doing my best to roll the 'R' in proper Hispanic manner but failing miserably. The kids giggled again, and Eddie rolled his eyes.

"Well, I decided to give my new knee a nickname too. I shortened its technical name to just plain Art.

"When I set off alarms at airports now, I just whip out a picture I carry in my wallet with photos of my loved ones. 'That's just Art, my extroverted knee. He likes attention.' Some officials actually laugh.

I turned to Mr. Macho and asked how badly his broken leg had hurt.

"Well," he admitted, "the pain really throbbed and wouldn't stop. I couldn't put any weight on it, so I couldn't even walk."

"I know just how you felt." I sympathized. "It is a good thing they didn't tell me too much about what to expect after my knee replacement. It hurt more than anything I imagined, but I was warned sternly that I couldn't, I repeat, COULD NOT lay around holding it still while it healed.

"There is a short window of time before scar tissue locks it into place. Whatever range of motion I had gained when that occurs is what I would have the rest of my days.

"In addition, there is no amount of pain medication that I could take that would completely obliterate the agony my physical therapist would inflict on me at each session. My PT gleefully referred to herself as a 'Physical Terrorist.'"

Not a particularly humorous title, but the room erupted in laughter anyway.

"Eventually, the grueling ordeal began to pay off. As I worked, cried, and prayed through it, the invasive entry began to close. Sinews and ligaments wrapped themselves around the foreign object like loving hugs. Blood vessels resumed their life-sustaining action. Even the nerves started to tingle again with new purpose. It started to feel just as real as the rest of me.

"Well, is it? It got me thinking, *What does it mean to be REAL?*

"I thought about that movie (you know the one) where Christians suddenly disappear from this earth, shedding their clothes, their jewelry, their contact lenses, even the fillings in their teeth. Anything that was not 'original equipment' remained after they departed.

"Then I thought about the Borgs in the show Star Trek. I put my thumb and my pinky finger to Stacey's temple and robotically droned 'You will be assimilated. Resistance is futile.' Doctors do their best to make sure anything they insert during surgery, from a new organ to a manufactured part, will be *assimilated* by the body.

"Several people in my life have died because their bodies rejected such an implant. What is more, the rejection by the body didn't just make the *new* part die, it made the whole body suffer.

"So, it made me ask myself, *Is my new knee a REAL part of my body, or will it forever be a foreign object merely tolerated by my body as long as it proves useful to me?*

"The answer may lie in a description The Book gives us about the church being the Body of Christ (Ephesians 1:22–23) and how this Body is constantly to be welcoming new members (Romans 15:7). It seems obvious that we are to accept them and make them one of us even though they require attention we are not used to giving.

I flexed my new knee until my calf and thigh came together to make my point.

"If I was willing to endure the pain and effort it took to make Art a REAL part of my body, is it too much to ask that I do the same to accept newly received members into the Body of Christ?

"Though it took time, I LOVE my new knee. Art kneels in prayer without aching the way my old knee did. He bends to put me at eye-level with you boys and girls for our weekly message.

"Similarly, I LOVE welcoming new members into our church

body—especially when they bring more kids to the children's message.

"Accommodating their newness and adjusting to their peculiarities is like spiritual 'therapy'. It can be hard but, in the long run, it is worth it. If we don't 'reject' them, they will eventually fit and function so perfectly, we wonder how we ever got along without them! If that isn't proof that they have become REAL, I don't know what is."

And He put all things in subjection under His feet, and made Him head over all things to the church, which is His body, the fullness of Him who fills all in all. (Ephesians 1:22-23)

Therefore, accept one another, just as Christ also accepted us, for the glory of God. (Romans 15:7)

Speaking the truth in love, we are to grow up in all aspects into Him who is the head, that is, Christ, from whom the whole body, being fitted and held together by what every joint supplies, according to the proper working of each individual part, causes the growth of the body for the building up of itself in love. (Ephesians 4:15-16)

They have lost connection with the head, from whom the whole body, supported and held together by its ligaments and sinews, grows as God causes it to grow. (Colossians 2:19, NIV)

Chapter THIRTY-FIVE
THE NAME OF MY GOD

Thirty-six years after a drunk driver nearly severed my leg, it was time for a 'tune up' on my knee. As do so many incidents in my life, it provided an anecdote for the next children's message.

"Have any of you had to go to the hospital?" Apparently, this is a status symbol as several of the kids clustered around me began waving their hands, excitedly.

I knew they wanted to share their experience before a captive audience, but there wasn't time, so I took the question to the next level. "Did you have to have *surgery*?"

All the hands went down except one.

"Did it hurt, and was it scary to watch?"

"I didn't get to see it." she admitted, "I fell asleep and don't remember anything about it. They gave me lots of ice cream when I woke up though."

The rest of the kids groaned jealously.

"Ah—must have been a tonsillectomy!" I diagnosed. She nodded, proud that her surgery had a big official title.

"A fancy word that means expensive," said her mom, rolling her eyes in the third row of the congregation.

"Don't I know it! Last week I told you about Art, my new knee. Today I want to tell you about something that happened the day of my knee surgery that almost made me change my mind." I paused as the kids leaned in, curious about what had happened.

"I thought about hopping right off the table and running away but I was wearing one of those hospital gowns that doesn't cover your hiney," I confided, dropping my voice to a whisper.

They were all appropriately appalled at the embarrassing prospect.

"My surgery was scheduled first thing in the morning, and the nurses went about the preparation very efficiently. I was instructed to don that obscene little hospital gown and to drink a mild sedative. They recorded my blood pressure and my pulse and told me that the surgeon would be in to see me before we began.

"When he arrived, he uncovered my knee, examined it, explained to me how the surgery would be performed, and pointed to each place he would be making an incision. Then he left to scrub up, and the nurses returned to take me to the procedure room.

"The nurse stared down at my still uncovered knee. 'Is *this* the knee?'

"I looked up to see if she was joking, but she was absolutely serious. Horror stories of botched surgeries done on the wrong limbs flashed through my mind, so I quickly assured her it was the correct knee.

"She sighed with exasperation which did not fill me with the confidence I needed to put my unconscious self in this medical team's hands.

"What's wrong?" I squeaked.

"He forgot to sign it," she said.

"Excuse me?" I sputtered.

"The doctor is required to initial the limb after his examination to authenticate his intention. I will have to go and get him," she replied, trying to mask her irritation. That was the moment I thought about jumping off the table!

"True to her word, she returned shortly with a sheepish doctor in tow. Handing him a pen, she watched as he signed his name on my knee. Then she lifted the gown from my other knee, upon which he wrote the word "NO."

"Satisfied at last, she allowed him to return to his scrubbing, and wheeled me away to be soundly sleeping in the operating room at his return.

"You all know the story in The Book about David killing Goliath with his slingshot, but do you remember how he got to be so good using it?"

"He was a shepherd, and that was how he protected his flock," one of them ventured.

"Uh huh, and that is where he was the day a prophet named Samuel was sent to show everyone who God wanted to be Israel's next king.

"Samuel went down the line of candidates standing before him, finally settling on one of David's brothers who had a royal look about him!

"He was about to announce his choice when The Book says the Lord told him he had the wrong guy. Samuel was understandably confused until he learned that one of the candidates was missing from the lineup.

"A servant was sent to bring the shepherd boy David back to see Samuel, and God said, 'that's the one!' He wasn't perfect but he was God's perfect choice to be king.

"To this day, God does not look at our appearance but at our hearts. He autographs those who belong to Him with His name, and nothing can steal what bears His seal.

"My son has a whole album of baseball cards, but he keeps an autographed Ken Griffey Jr. card in a protective case in a locked drawer. Why does he do that?

The kids and adults answered together in awed unison, "Because it is valuable!"

That wave of peer envy worked right into my zinger.

"Well, as it happens, I have an autograph that is even bigger and better, and I bet you do too." I was instantly rewarded with their complete attention.

"When my doctor wrote his name on me, it washed away in just a few days. But the God we worship, the same God who is King of the Universe, the author and creator of EVERYTHING including The Book, put His autograph on me and you and *you* and YOU," I announced loudly sweeping the room with my arms.

"Not only that, He used a permanent marker. Can you just imagine how *valuable* that makes us?

"Eventually, He intends to keep those who have His name written on them with Him forever. His Divine autograph will be the indelible proof about who goes with Him into His heavenly temple and, sadly, who does not."

The one who overcomes, I will make him a pillar in the temple of My God, and he will not go out from it anymore; and I will write on him the name of My God...(Revelation 3:12a)

But the LORD said to Samuel, "Do not look at his appearance or at the height of his stature, because I have rejected him; for God does not see as man sees, since man looks at the outward appearance, but the LORD looks at the heart." (1 Samuel 16:7)

Chapter
THIRTY-SIX

A
PEAR-ABLE

I thought I had the best children's message prop I had ever come up with and was anticipating a lot of amusement watching the kids scratch their heads and ponder the riddle I was about to spring on them.

As about twenty kids crowded around me, I drew a one-liter glass bottle with a narrow neck from my bag and held it up for all to see. Inside the bottle was a beautiful, perfectly formed, fully ripened pear. The bottle had been filled to the brim with a clear liquid, and then corked.

I had counted on a lengthy period of puzzled scrutiny as they looked for signs of container tampering, a carefully glued opening, or perhaps a trick bottom. I even held it high enough to encourage the participation of the adult onlookers.

"How do you suppose that pear got inside the bottle?" I asked, taking the direct approach.

From somewhere in the middle of the pack, somebody threw up their hands and I heard, "Oh, I don't know! Maybe it grew in there!"

I was *discombobulated*, to say the least. Yep, that's what I was! I was used to, intentionally, letting the kids outsmart me in my weekly interaction with them but one-upping me when I wasn't expecting it was definitely discombobulating!

I took advantage of the knee-slapping laughter going on in the room to compose myself so I could spin my parable—or maybe that should be 'pear-able'.

I shaded my eyes a bit as I scanned my group to try and pinpoint the answer's origin, without success, and then began my allegory. "Well, that was fast," I peevishly lamented, "But you are absolutely right!

"When the pear tree was still in blossom, my folks had pushed several bottles over the budding branches of the pear trees in their orchard. That pear had literally grown inside the bottle. When the pears were harvested that fall, they snapped the pear from its branch by gently pulling the bottle away, then poured a preservative solution inside and sealed it. That was over forty years ago. I still have the bottle today, and that pear looks just as fresh and delicious as it did when I first saw it.

"My husband, who was an atheist until God got his attention at the age of 25, has told me many times about how much he envies that I have never known a day when I was not a Christian. I cannot tell you the date and time that I accepted Jesus as my Savior. I just always knew that He was. I have no dramatic conversion story to tell, just a complete and overwhelming assurance that's been there my whole life.

"I'm kind of like that pear in the bottle. When I was just an embryo, my parents prayed for me. When I was born, they vowed to raise me completely protected by the all-encompassing love of my Creator.

"As I grew, I was surrounded by others who were growing just as I was. Some were encased in the secure environment of their own safe bottles—fellow Christians.

"Many around me were growing wild, dangling freely, hanging on for dear life, at the mercy of the elements. My husband had wonderful parents who did everything they could to teach their sons morals and ethics so I can't say he was growing wild, BUT in his owns words, he said he ENVIED me because I had always been sure I had a Creator who loved me, a Savior who redeemed me, and a Spirit who guided me every day.

"Some individuals, like pears that our cows found lying on the ground below their trees, were blown from their branches prematurely. I grew up near a logging town, so being "blown from branches prematurely" is a fitting analogy. I lost more friends to accidents in that *extremely dangerous* field of work than I did friends serving their country in the Vietnam War. But the point is, this life ends in death, no matter how it happens.

"Others might make it to harvest season. But what then? Let's look back at my husband one more time. His family was in a very serious car accident when he was five. He almost died. His mother went into premature labor with his little brother, and they both almost died. His father lost his guitar-picking thumb but was so numb with grief over what was happening to his family, he didn't care. Then, guess what?"

The kids had been absolutely silent as I spoke, but their faces were a sea of emotion. *Death* is a topic that, unfortunately, in the Church is always considered "outside the box" but, over the years, the kids (and their parents) had come to trust me with it.

"They ALL survived!" The kids' faces relaxed with relief! "Because it was not yet their 'harvest season,' God patiently waited for them to seek and find Him as they went on to hang on for dear life through many more of the scary experiences we all have in life.

"When someone who did not believe they needed a Savior to preserve them for the life after this one has died, I mourn their passing. I am sad because I've lost them forever. When someone who has let Jesus 'fit them for heaven to live with Him there'* I am sad because I miss them but I do not mourn for them. I know they have begun their eternal life and I will see them again.

"What do you kids think of the story in The Book about Jesus healing a blind man's sight by spitting in the dirt and then smearing the mud he made all over the man's eyes" (John 9:6)? I was rewarded with various degrees of revulsion but I had my 'gotcha' ready.

"The Book says God told Adam, 'I made you out of dust and your body is going to go back where it came from' (Genesis 3:19, paraphrased). Maybe Jesus was just applying a little more of the same material God used originally on the man's eyes to repair a malfunctioning body part.

After a split second of stunned silence, the whole room erupted with knee slaps and hand claps. I had to shush them so I could continue.

"I don't know what the earthly life ahead holds for me, and you don't know what it holds for you. What I do know is that, when I die, I will be preserved forever." The Book says that includes our spirit, our soul, and our body (I Thessalonians 5:23, paraphrased). But if our bodies are going to return to the dust, how is that possible?

I scratched my head along with them and then went on with a big smile.

"The Book says our risen Savior's power has no limits. Everything is subjected to Him, and He will transform our forever bodies so they are no longer made of earthly sod but of the glory of God (Philippians 3:20-21).

I held my evidence tightly with both hands and raised it slowly until every face in the room had to turn upward to keep it in their field of vision.

"If you continue to let your *faith family* surround you as you grow and ripen, you will hear pastors remind you of that whenever you receive this blessing:

'The body and blood of our Lord strengthen and PRESERVE you in the true faith to LIFE EVERLASTING.'

"Like that pear in its bottle, only better!"

You are a hiding place for me; you preserve me from trouble; you surround me with shouts of deliverance. (Psalm 32:7)

May the God of peace himself sanctify you completely. May your whole spirit, soul, and body be preserved blameless at the coming of our Lord Jesus Christ. (1 Thessalonians 5:23, WEB)

For our citizenship is in heaven, from which we also eagerly wait for a Savior, the Lord Jesus Christ; who will transform the body of our lowly condition into conformity with His glorious body, by the exertion of the power that He has even to subject all things to Himself. (Philippians 3:20-21)

* Be near me, Lord Jesus; I ask Thee to stay
close by me forever, and love me, I pray.
Bless all the dear children in Thy tender care,
and fit us for heaven, to live with Thee there.
(Christmas Carol AWAY IN A MANGER, verse 3)

Chapter
THIRTY-SEVEN

NEENER, NEENER, NEENER

"Dying is as normal as being born," I said as I looked out over the congregation. "But that doesn't keep it from hurting a lot to lose someone you love."

I sat down on the steps with the kids and put my arm around the closest one and hugged her to me. This was a challenging topic, but I wanted to make it real.

"Never being able to hug them again, see them, talk to them, just seems so *final*. The Book tells us Jesus cried over the death of his friend Lazarus—even though he knew he was about to prove to his followers that death was *not* final!

"Missing a person who dies still hurts even when we know that there is an eternal world after this one. But how many of you have lost a pet?"

Hands raised, and faces sobered.

"When we buried a beloved pet on the family farm a few years ago, I wasn't so sure if the same is true for animals. Is he gone for good...or just for now?

"We were somewhat skeptical when our daughter BrieDanielle added him to our pet menagerie, but it wasn't long before her handsome "Rotty" named Hershey proved to be a gentle giant with a big heart. Even our cats curled up with him at bedtime."

Hunter nodded when I asked, "Do you remember riding on Hershey's back from your house to ours just like Madeline did in the *Good Dog, Carl* stories?

"Actually, you all got to know and love him one Christmas when he was dressed as a shepherd in our Christmas Pageant.

The kids laughed at the recollection of a potbelly pig among the Nativity sheep one year and a couple of chickens pretending to be doves on the stable roof.

I chuckled with them. "Yes, our performances are always improvised with whatever is available, animals included.

"Hershey was my cooking companion, ready to clean up anything that fell to the floor," I recalled glumly.

"And he loved to have his haunches scratched." I illustrated it with a vigorous ten-finger clawing motion. "He would purposefully, back up to me and practically sit on my knees until I obliged. Afterwards, he would reward me with a footbath, covering every inch of my bare tootsies with his wet kisses.

"It was a sad day when he took his last breath. My daughter thought we should each do something in his memory, so I went 'outside the box' and had a tiny Hershey's Kiss tattooed on one of the feet he used to bathe.

"It is quite normal and natural to grieve and honor the dead; elaborate funerals with gold-plated caskets, scattering ashes in meaningful locations so, yes, even tattoos. I don't know of any culture that does not have a mourning ritual or service. Pets take up a lot of real estate in our hearts, so mourning them after they die is to be expected.

"There are those who tell me animals have no souls and do not go to heaven. Maybe that's true, but The Book also mentions the wolf and the lamb getting along together in the new heaven and earth. And, don't forget that Jesus rides a white horse. Sure sounds like animals will be there!

"I have often envisioned my first day in heaven; meeting saints I had dreamed of talking with and loved ones who had gone on long before, then seeing Hershey come bounding over a green hill to give me kisses.

"I really don't know the answer about animals going to heaven." I threw up my hands at this point and shook my head slowly. "And I don't think anyone else does either.

"What I do know for sure, is that there is only *one* way to find out," I said, raising an index finger in emphasis, "and it's NOT by honoring those who have died, but serving the One who died for ME and for YOU and YOU and YOU."

As my finger rested on individuals while I spoke, the kids themselves started a tiny little wave of pointing that grew until it circled the sanctuary. I am sure God was smiling.

"When God raised Jesus back to life He even gloated over the win. The Book quotes in First Corinthians: '*WHERE, O DEATH, IS YOUR VICTORY? WHERE, O DEATH, IS YOUR STING?*' That sentence is kind of like '*neener neener neener!*'.

The children all took up the familiar chant for a few seconds, so I crossed my arms and let them wind down on their own. I was thinking it was the perfect takeaway from the hardest topic we had ever dealt with.

"We know without a shadow of a doubt that for humans, Jesus is the Way to eternal life in the presence of the Creator of all things. Still, in The Book, Jesus also assures us that not even the death of a bird escapes His notice. So maybe, *just maybe,* we'll see all our beloved animals in heaven.

Jesus said to him, "I am the way, and the truth, and the life; no one comes to the Father except through Me." (John 14:6)

Therefore when Jesus saw [Mary] weeping, and the Jews who came with her also weeping, He was deeply moved in spirit and was troubled, and He said, Where have you laid him?" They said to Him, "Lord, come and see." Jesus wept. (John 11:33-35)

Where, O Death, is your victory? Where, O Death, is your sting? (1 Corinthians 15:55)

And the wolf will dwell with the lamb, And the leopard will lie down with the young goat, And the calf and the young lion and the fattened steer will be together; And a little boy will lead them. (Isaiah 11:6)

And I saw heaven opened, and behold, a white horse, and He who sat on it is called Faithful and True, and in righteousness He judges and wages war. (Revelation 19:11)

Are five sparrows not sold for two assaria? And yet not one of them has gone unnoticed in the sight of God. (Luke 12:6)

Chapter
THIRTY-EIGHT

IF GOD IS
IN CONTROL

M y eclectic collection of coffee mugs is as random as the chapters in this book, and I mourn when one of my favorites gets broken. A chip in the rim is enough to make me, reluctantly, throw it away. A sip and a chip do not go together even if they do rhyme!

Many of the mugs contain thematic messages, and I rummage through them to find one that fits my mood of the day. One says, "God answers all prayer. Sometimes He says, 'yes,' sometimes He says 'no,' and sometimes He says, 'You've got to be kidding!' " Another one says, "Dear God, I'm giving it my best."

Another one I used to use frequently reminded me each time I raised it to my lips that "GOD IS IN CONTROL." One day, I was irritated to find that mug in the kitchen sink with, you guessed it, a big chunk missing from the rim. It was on its way to the trash when a thought hit me, "Well, if God is in control, why did He break my mug?"

Then I began to recall countless tragedies where the overall reaction was just that: "If God is in control, why did He let this happen?"

The Tsunami in 2004, Katrina, Haiti, 9-11, four police officers gunned down in a coffee shop, a child hit by a drunk driver, a young mother with small children dying of breast cancer, even the untimely death of a beloved pet are just a few examples I have heard from non-believers AND even from Christians.

In fact, one that surfaced just recently was a non-Christian who said, "How can you call your God loving when he even let his own son be killed?"

When I hear people who don't believe in God blame a god they don't believe in for things that happen, it is enough to make me bang my head against the wall.

Consider the US Airways flight whose 155 passengers were spared when Captain "Sully" landed the jet in the middle of the Hudson River. Condensed newspaper highlights reported:

> ...flight's pilot, C.B. Sullenberger, emerges as hero of "miracle on the Hudson" with praise being heaped on him by passengers, officials, and aviation experts. "I don't think there's enough praise to go around for someone who does something like this. This is something you really can't prepare for," said former Delta pilot Denny Walsh. The President says he is inspired by skill, heroism of flight crew, rescue teams. (CNN)

Isn't it ironic that when things go terribly wrong, God gets blamed, but when tragedy is averted or the story has a happy ending, another hero is given the credit?

After a harrowing road trip in stormy conditions, I arrived at a destination murmuring "thank you, Lord." The driver, who had not known me very long, turned and shot me a disgusted glare, to which I reacted with, "Don't you just hate it when you do the work, and God gets the credit?"

He considered that for a second and then said, sheepishly, "well, there were a couple of times back there when I kind of think He might have helped."

"Really? You were praying too?" I asked.

"No," he countered, blasphemously, "not unless you count 'Jesus Christ, watch it!' when that car cut in on me or 'Oh My God!' when we spun out on the ice."

"Maybe the Lord thought you were trying to strike up a conversation," I laughed, "After all, you not only called on Him, you acted like He was familiar to you. You know, like my dad, my boss, my friend." I smiled, innocently.

Even Christians can be quite adept at micro-managing God. We may not call out His name in vain, but we tend to keep Him as our back-up plan, not our pre-set GPS.

Consider God's predicament. We try it our way. We screw up. We call on Him in a panic and then blame Him if He doesn't fix, get, or do it for us.

He is the ultimate father. If He never allows us to suffer any consequences, we will never learn from our actions. Even the natural disasters that befall innocent people are the consequences of a world crumbling around us because our original parents pretty much let God know they wanted to be in control.

More times than I can count, people have told me, "The Bible says God will never give you more than you can handle." I've been through The Book cover to cover several times, and I have never found that statement. Well-meaning folk might be referring to a passage (1 Corinthians 10:13) that says that God will not let you be **tempted** beyond what you have the ability to say "no" to, and that He will provide a way out of the temptation.

The truth is, God will ALWAYS let you experience more than you can handle, with the promise He will be right there to PROVIDE help when you genuinely let Him be in control.

That chipped mug did not go in the trash. I keep it as a reminder that not everything is God's fault. Sometimes we humans have only ourselves to blame for actions that happen in a world we insist on controlling.

When all is said and done, The Book says EVERY knee will bow to God. Letting Him be in control of our lives now sure seems like a better choice than being forced to kneel later.

No temptation has overtaken you except something common to mankind; and God is faithful, so He will not allow you to be tempted beyond what you are able, but with the temptation will provide the way of escape also, so that you will be able to endure it. (1 Corinthians 10:13)

For it is written: "AS I LIVE, SAYS THE LORD, TO ME EVERY KNEE WILL BOW, AND EVERY TONGUE WILL GIVE PRAISE TO GOD." (Romans 14:11)

Chapter
THIRTY-NINE

BIRD-WATCHING

"**D**o any of you have pet birds?" I asked the kids sprawled on the floor in front of me.

"What kind of bird do you have?" I prompted the only one who raised his hand. He said it was a parakeet named Pete and that there been two of them but one died.

"That's sad, I'm sorry." I went on. "Do you keep Pete in a cage?"

"Yeah, but we let him out to fly around the room. I play a game with him sometimes."

"What kind of a game can you play with a bird?" I was genuinely interested.

"Well, he perches on my finger, and I stick my tongue out and wiggle it. It drives him crazy!"

"Does he peck at your tongue?" I was really interested now.

"No, from his hopping up and down on my finger and chirping, I think he is scared of it. Afterwards, I pet him and scratch under his wings to calm him down. I am pretty sure he thinks I have saved him from the monster, and he loves me like I am his hero."

His story set everyone to laughing, and I waited a few minutes to go on.

"Well, my birds are not what I would call pets. They are a pair of ravens that have hung out in my woods for several years now. They are very large with a wingspan bigger than a yardstick." I held my arms out wide so they could get the idea.

"Every day I perch some pieces I think they might like on a fence rail close to my compost pile. They have gotten to be very spoiled and will often come closer to the house to tell me they are hungry.

"In The Book, the disciples were worried about where their next meal and tunic were going to come from if they left their jobs to follow Jesus. He told them to 'consider the ravens' who never worry about such things and yet their heavenly Father feeds them."

"I know I don't HAVE to feed my ravens because Jesus said God would take care of it, but I like to do it. They are a constant reminder to me to consider how God takes care of them and how I am much more valuable to Father God than they are. If I start to get anxious about having my worldly needs met, I just say to myself, 'Consider the ravens.'

"On the other hand, on the days that I plow through the snow or slosh through the rain to give them their treats, I remind *them* that their day to return the favor may be coming! The Book tells us that God sent ravens to feed Elijah when his country was suffering from a drought."

I thought they would find that amusing but from the appalled looks on their faces I had guessed wrong. "What?" I rebounded. "It was God's idea, not mine!"

"Well, we have a little time left so I want to tell you another bird story."

I pulled a chubby stuffed turtle out of my bag and set it down on the floor.

"That's not a bird!" they chorused.

"No, but this is," I said, putting my hand into an elaborate eagle puppet. "I heard one of Aesop's fables slightly revised at a graduation ceremony and I have never forgotten it.

"Once upon a time, a turtle plodding along on the ground saw an eagle fly down and land on a treetop nearby. 'Boy, I sure wish I could fly like you.' He called out.

" 'Well,' said, the eagle, 'How about I give you a lift?' "

With that, I let my eagle puppet swoop down and, with the help of a little Velcro on the claws, pick up the turtle on the floor before me. I lifted them high above my head and went on.

" 'Wow,' said the turtle, 'this is the coolest thing ever!' About that time the eagle felt a little movement from the turtle and looked down. He saw the turtle's little, tiny flippers waving madly.

" 'What are you doing?' asked the eagle.

" 'I am flying!' said the turtle.

" 'You are NOT flying,' the eagle retorted. 'I am carrying you!'

" 'No, no!' said the turtle. 'I have been watching you very closely and I think I have the hang of it now,' and he flapped his useless little feet again."

The kids chortled at the ridiculous idea.

"The eagle tried again. 'I am telling you the truth; you are NOT flying!'

" 'Yes I am! You can let go now.'

" 'But, but...' sputtered the eagle.

" 'But nothing, you tyrant. Let me go!

" 'Okay,' sighed the eagle as he let the turtle plummet helplessly to the earth."

Reaching up, I pulled the turtle free from my eagle's claws and let it drop to the floor with a thud. The startled kids all jumped at the realization that the turtle was no more.

I knelt down on their level, using my puppeteer power to keep the eagle's wings fluttering as gracefully as I could as I left them with a spiritual moral I hoped they would take to heart.

"As you go through life, ALWAYS remember that your heavenly Father is the provider of all your worldly needs, and the source of all your strength and of all your abilities. If you trust Him, he will carry you and NEVER let go, forever guarding your days and guiding your ways."

...Do not worry about your life, as to what you are to eat; nor for your body, as to what you are to wear. For life is more than food, and the body is more than clothing. Consider the ravens, that they neither sow nor reap; they have no storeroom nor barn, and yet God feeds them; how much more valuable you are than the birds! (Luke 12:22–24)

Then the word of the LORD came to Elijah....You will drink from the brook, and I have directed the ravens to supply you with food there. So he did what the LORD had told him....The ravens brought him bread and meat in the morning and bread and meat in the evening, and he drank from the brook. (1 Kings 17:2–6, NIV)

With his feathers he will cover you, under his wings you will find safety. His truth is your shield and armor. (Psalm 91:4)

Chapter
FORTY

BOTANY
FOR DUMMIES

Yesterday I thought "what this rainy weekend could use is some cheering up." So, I went to the local florist to pick up the twelve dozen daffodils I had ordered to make a massive bright display on the church altar.

When the clerk handed me a rather puny box I thought, "This can't possibly have 144 flowers in it." I opened it and was shocked to discover twelve tightly bound bundles of unopened buds.

I looked at her with dismay. "No, I need twelve dozen OPEN flowers for tomorrow morning." Smiling, she assured me, "Honey, if you put these in warm water overnight, they will be open by morning."

"How warm is warm?" I shot back.

"Cool enough that you can still put your hand in it but not lukewarm; definitely on the warm side of warm," she specified.

I was more than dubious, but I appeared to have no choice. I made my purchase and took the box of flowers-to-be to the church, where I set them on the altar in twelve vases full of water that was definitely on the warm side of warm.

The next morning when I arrived early for choir warm-up, sure enough, they were open. The daffodils drooped down over the vases like a massive trumpet section...all mournfully playing the blues on the surface of the altar. The blossoms were gorgeous! The stems, on the other hand, had been reduced to wilted slime.

I spent the next hour cutting the ruined stalks off the heads and inserted the nubs into straws from the church kitchen. As I stood them up in the vases, I thought, "There is a children's message in here somewhere."

Later, as the kids came forward, I asked them if they liked the beautiful display on the altar. I was holding two thumbs up and got nods of enthusiastic approval. Then I turned my two thumbs down and began my explanation.

"I had originally thought that each of you could take some of the flowers home for your moms after the service, but there was a little problem," I sighed.

Holding up a couple of droopy examples still attached to their soggy stems, I proceeded to tell them what had happened. I showed them the makeshift remedy that had been used. "I guess my hands are used to warmer water than the lady who gave me the advice," I told them. "I think I got it too hot!"

When everybody stopped laughing, I waved my hand toward the altar and said, "I took drastic steps to produce this glorious display but, sadly, it will not even last through the day. The straws can hold the flowers up indefinitely, but the life-giving source of water is gone. They will be dead and dry before the sun goes down.

"You know, sometimes when we get impatient and try to take God's matters into our own hands, we can really get ourselves into hot water." I let that sink in until I got a few grins. "That is not to say that God can't use us anyway, but sometimes He has to take some pretty drastic steps to fix the messes we make.

"His fixes are not temporary, like my poor efforts to salvage the disaster of my good intentions, though. Think about it," I said, holding up one of the straws holding a daffodil, "as pretty as they are, these flowers were already dying when I bought them at the florist. I just helped them get there sooner.

"God's fixes, on the other hand, are life-giving. As long as we stay rooted in Him, He pours His love out in our hearts. God showers us with blessings like thirst-quenching, crop-nourishing rain until we receive His biggest blessing of all, Life Eternal."

I pointed out the sanctuary windows at the dreary downpour pounding the parking lot. "It might not seem like it, but those raindrops are a blessing in disguise. When our Pacific NW rain goes on for days or even weeks it can be pretty depressing, but we know it has a happy ending.

"I have a big barrel on my patio with a rosebush in it. Sometimes I forget to water it and, when I notice it looking kind of wilted, I hurry to give it a good soaking. But, to my surprise, the water I pour in the container just sits on top of the dirt. It doesn't soak down into the roots like I want it to. It has to wait until the ground itself becomes saturated.

"The Book reminds us that ground that drinks the rain that often falls on it is actually blessed by God. Now, if ground that gets rained on OFTEN doesn't describe western Washington, I don't know what does. But while we are sloshing through puddles and shaking off our umbrellas, the soaked ground is sending God's rain to the roots of the vegetation that brings us such spirit-lifting joy when its blooms appear."

I made a slow turn with the finger that was pointing out the window toward the altar. Everyone's eyes followed my finger until their vision was filled with the array of the first golden flowers of spring completely covering the altar. "A blessing from God," I whispered.

The grass withers, the flower fades, but the word of our God stands forever. (Isaiah 40:8)

But whoever drinks of the water that I will give him shall never be thirsty; but the water that I will give him will become in him a fountain of water springing up to eternal life. (John 4:14)

For ground that drinks the rain which often falls on it and produces vegetation useful to those for whose sake it is also tilled, receives a blessing from God; (Hebrews 6:7)

"We have a special guest with us today. All the way from Ireland!" I pointed over to the worship team where Patrick was going to be adding his fiddle to the morning's accompaniment.

The kids all waved at him, and he waved his bow back at them with a smile.

"I'm going to start us off with a question. Feel free to just blurt out the answer. What does 'The Mountain is Out' mean?"

That was much too easy.

"You can see Mount Rainier," the entire room thundered in unison.

"A 14,000-foot snowy peak less than 60 miles from urban Seattle makes a pretty impressive neighbor—when you can see it. It's hard to imagine that the gloomy gray clouds drenching the Pacific Northwest with rain can hide something that big, but they do.

"I was taking the Amtrak from Portland to Seattle one day when I overheard a conversation behind me among some tourists from California sightseeing the coast by train. Their self-appointed tour guide was, at that moment pointing west where, in the distance, the Olympic Mountains jutted up from the Olympic Peninsula of Washington.

"'Over there,' he said, confidently, 'Is Mount Rainier.' The whole group began to lift their cameras.

"I couldn't just sit there! Turning around with a smile, I said, 'Excuse me! Before you snap that picture, you might want to know that is NOT Mount Rainier.'

"The spokesman of the group was not quite ready to concede his error.

" But, the Guide in the seat pocket says we should be seeing Mount Rainier at this point.'

" 'Yes, you should!' I agreed. By this time, I wasn't just smiling, I was chuckling. 'Just look over your right shoulder.' The whole group swiveled in that direction and, what do you suppose the reaction was?"

The expectant church crowd before me jumped when I yelled, "AACK!"

"Yep," I grinned. "All of the Californians jumped like you just did when Mount Rainier suddenly filled their entire vision, almost as if it was on the train with them.

" 'Now, when you catch your breath and stop clutching your chests,' I said to the group on the train, 'You are going to want to snap some pictures, probably in panoramic mode.'

"I watched them taking each other's photos with the base of the mountain spanning all of the windows on the east side of the train behind them as they posed. Yep, the Mountain was out in all its glory!

"It has been a little disappointing that Patrick has not gotten to see our mountain during his visit. So, this morning on my way to church, I took a few pictures of Mount Rainier for him to remember it by and had them downloaded to our media screen."

I clicked the remote on the projector and up popped my first shot; a completely gray blur with a few raindrops spattering my windshield filled the screen.

Everybody laughed, including Patrick. "Yeah," I punned, "today is 'rain-ier' than I had hoped but I did my best. Here, I took a couple more, so we would have several to choose from." Another driz-zly shot hit the screen "Patrick, if you like, I can have one of these framed for you to take home."

As the kids pondered my group of misty gray photos, Jocelyne finally broke the ice.

"But you can't see the mountain!"

"But we've seen it before, so we know it's there, right?" I paused to let them mull that over.

"But *Patrick* hasn't seen it before," one of them finally said with exasperation.

I looked over at Patrick.

"Hmm, well I guess he will just have to take our word for it. Let's find out." I pointed at the screen and continued as if I was a lawyer approaching the jury box.

"Pat, do you believe Mount Rainier is in these pictures even if you can't see it?"

He nodded emphatically, never taking his eyes off the screen.

"Why do you believe it if you can't see it?"

"Because you told me it is! Just because the Mountain is NOT Out, doesn't mean it's not there," he explained in his heavy Irish brogue.

"Patrick's candid logic perfectly illustrates something Jesus said to one of his disciples in The Book. Thomas refused to believe Je-sus had been raised from the dead unless he could actually see and touch him personally.

"Suddenly, he found himself face to face with the living Lord, who was inviting him to touch the wounds in his hands and side if that is what believing was going to take.

"We don't hear much about most of the twelve disciples, but even two thousand years later when we hear someone called a 'doubting Thomas' we remember this one.

"Some people are just pessimistic by nature, and they take more convincing to get on board. When they finally get it, their belief is just as strong as their unbelief was. In fact, they will be just the ones God can use to reach fellow skeptics. They are qualified to say, 'Yeah, that's how I was too.'

"Patrick, on the other hand, shows us what it is like to believe without needing extra convincing! The Book says *Happy are they*! I nodded to our pleased Irishman, who proved my point with a grin. 'Just look at that smiling face over there!'"

Jesus said to him, "Because you have seen Me, have you now believed? Blessed (happy) are they who did not see, and yet believed. (John 20:29)

Chapter
FORTY-TWO
DE DEBIL MADE ME DO IT

"There used to be a popular cartoon showing a devil sitting on someone's shoulder coaxing, 'Go ahead, do it,' and an angel sitting on the other shoulder whispering 'You know it's wrong! Don't do it.'" I studied the neatly dressed and combed kids sitting in front of me, assessing their reaction to that mental image.

"The Book tells us that God gave us the ability to tell right from wrong. It's a part of our very being, what we call our *conscience*.

"When you find yourself wishing you had not done something bad, it means you know you made the wrong choice. You have what is called a 'guilty conscience'.

"When my husband was a little boy, he was allowed to walk to a local market with a list of groceries his mom needed. One day, while the grocer was gathering up the items on her list, he slipped a pack of gum into his pocket." Some kids fidgeted, and others frowned. I paused with a loud sigh and that seemed to make them even more uncomfortable.

"On his way home, he was so overcome with guilt he could not even bring himself to open the pack. His mom was a well-respected teacher in the school district, and he was concerned that she might lose her job if anyone found out what he had done.

"His conscience was telling him he had done wrong. The next time he was sent to the store, he worked up enough courage to take the little pack of gum out of his pocket and hand it to the store owner.

"The grocer smiled at him and said, 'Billy, I saw you take the gum,' and, as Billy hung his head in shame, he continued, 'but I had a feeling you would be back to make it right.'" A few shoulders relaxed as if the kids were relieved the story had a happily ever after. "Do you know, he has never in his whole life forgotten about it? But just as sharp in his memory is the fact that, when he 'fessed up to what he had done, his sin had been forgiven by the neighborhood grocer!" One little girl clapped, enthusiastically, and then quickly stopped, realizing no one had joined her.

Then I switched gears, scrutinizing my line-up of suspects like a detective.

"How many of you were in Sunday School this morning?" That was a simple call to action. All the hands went up. "So, what was today's snack?"

"Popcorn!" was the quick reply.

My innocent chitchat had led them into a false sense of security that I was about to spoil.

"I thought so because there is a huge trail of popcorn all over the floor in the fellowship hall." Eyes widened but mouths were, suspiciously, closed.

I crossed my arms. "No one wants to volunteer who made the mess?"

I heard one small giggle, and then someone went "Shhh!" Again, silence.

"Hmmm. If I ask my kids who did something or made a mess you know what they say?"

About a dozen moms in the room exclaimed "*Not Me!*"

It was hard to keep my interrogator demeanor and not laugh. "Wow! *Not Me* sure gets around. Apparently, that sneaky sinner doesn't just hang out at my house!

"We can blame *Not Me* all we want, but The Book tells us that our guilty conscience is going to keep making us feel really bad until we admit that we did something wrong and say we're sorry. Nothing feels good because that one bad thing is stuck in our conscience. Why do we let that wreck our good times? Especially since The Book says we get rewarded for 'fessing up to our sin. Not just one reward but three!

"First, when the confession is hardly out of our mouths, we get compassion. Instead of punishment, we find kindness.

"Second, we get forgiveness. God forgives us because Jesus took our punishment for sin when He died on the cross. Then The Book says we MUST forgive each other to the same degree God forgave us.

"Third, we get a bath."

That brought the guilty faces that had been obstinately focused on their laps up to attention with a jumbled chorus of "huh?"

"It's right here in The Book," I defended. "It says we are cleansed from all unrighteousness. Soap and water, right?"

"Not quite," clarified one budding theologian. "I think it means cleaning inside. You know, like getting it out of our system."

"Hmm..." I tapped my chin, "That does make a lot more sense!"

"Now back to the popcorn mess. Who did it, and who should clean it up?" I scanned their eyes and continued. "In just a few minutes everybody in this sanctuary will be walking all over it while they fellowship in that room."

A few sheepish kids stood up, but before they could speak, the church custodian cleared his throat and made a completely unscripted comment from the doorway, "What about the rest of you? I saw you ALL throwing your popcorn up in the air and trying to catch it in your mouths. Fun, yes, but leaving the mess was very wrong."

What followed was an absolute din of 'I'm sorry confessions' followed by 'I will help clean it up right now,' accompanied by a general stampede toward the door.

Before they could leave the room though, the custodian stopped them with open arms and smiled. "It's all right. I forgive you, and you can go back to sit with your parents. I cleaned it up for you."

No day in any court could have ended with a spiritual life lesson that was more divinely appointed.

...they show the work of the Law written in their hearts, their conscience testifying and their thoughts alternately accusing or else defending them... (Romans 2:15)

If we confess our sins, He is faithful and righteous, so that He will forgive us our sins and cleanse us from all unrighteousness. (1 John 1:9)

One who conceals his wrongdoings will not prosper, but one who confesses and abandons them will find compassion. (Proverbs 28:13)

...put on a heart of compassion, kindness, humility, gentleness, and patience; bearing with one another, and forgiving each other...just as the Lord forgave you, so must you do also. (Colossians 3:12-13)

Chapter
FORTY-THREE

EAST
FROM WEST

"How many of you have seen *Back to the Future*?" All hands shot up like the movie's DeLorean taking flight.

"Anybody ever travel to the east coast and back?" That earned me another show of hands. "Do you know that qualifies you as a time traveler?" That really got their attention.

As I pointed east, I said, "When I fly coast to coast, from one Washington to the other, I might land at my dinner time, but the President might be putting on his jammies for bed." The kids nodded and giggled, their funny bones tickled.

Then I reversed the direction my fingers were pointing.

"But there are some trips a traveler could take from East to West and arrive BEFORE they left!" I imitated the sound of a tape re-winding.

One of my *time-travelers-in-training* added "Like Marty McFly!"

"Wouldn't it be great if we could rewind to BEFORE we sinned?" Heads nodded in both the pews and the congregation at my feet.

"As far as God is concerned when He forgives us, it never happened at all! IT'S LIKE WE WENT BACK TO THE FUTURE, the ultimate rewind.

"According to The Book, He completely erases our sin '*as far as the East is from the West.*' The distance between East and West can't be measured, because it has no end. The sun in its journey is constantly bringing us a brand new day."

I lifted one of the toddlers onto my lap. "Tell me," I asked, "What does your mom or dad do when you misbehave?" That earned me a "how did you know?" look.

I saw the parents leaning forward to hear the answer. The child, who was now squirming in my lap, whispered quietly, "I get a time-out."

"Did you get what you wanted?" Just a negative headshake this time. "In other words, they took the temptation away from you. Smart parents! Were you even a little bit sorry about how you acted?"

This time there were almost imperceptible nods from the *whole* group as if they were considering their own similar incidents. Setting the child back down, I said, "You DIDN'T get what you wanted, but do you know what you DID get?"

Even the older ones leaned in to hear my answer.

"You got a **'do-over'**! But here's the thing about 'do-overs'. It means you get another chance to make a right or wrong decision!

"Just last week we talked about how your conscience is like a good voice whispering in one ear and a bad voice whispering in the other ear."

One little boy blurted out, "Oh! I drew a picture this week of an angel with wings sitting on one shoulder and a devil with horns sitting on the other."

"Good job, Andrew! I looked toward each shoulder and tapped my ears. "You always have to decide which voice in your conscience you are going to listen to.

"I kind of wish I hadn't," Andrew retorted. "Mom hung it on the 'frigerator,' and now I see it every time I start to open the door without asking."

The kids around him nodded, sympathetically, while a couple of the moms in the congregation muttered, "I wish I had one of those on my 'frigerator.' "

"Yes, we earthly parents can do what it takes to give our little sinners a 'do-over' and let them try again," I confessed to my parental audience. "But sometimes I'm more inclined to record it in their Baby Books than forget about it."

That set the entire congregation clapping and laughing as my little group looked at each other, uneasily.

"It is SO, SO different with our Heavenly Father. If we are sorry, He doesn't just forgive and hope for the best, He wipes the slate completely clean like we are going *as far as the east is from the west* into a future where our sin hasn't happened yet! The Book tells us God's **do-over** gives us the chance to make sure it never happens at all!

"God does this through His son, Jesus, who was completely innocent because He *always* made His Father's choice. He took on the punishment for the things we know are wrong but do them anyway."

I covered my face with my hands and shook my head. "It makes me so ashamed to think how much it hurts Him every time I choose wrong over right."

About that time, I felt a comforting pat on my arm from one of my little cherubs who was looking at me, anxiously. All the little shoulders in my group relaxed as I reassured them with a smile, "If you always follow where God's SON leads, you get another chance to make the most of God's kind of do-over—the future kind that hasn't happened yet and never will if you keep going in the right direction."

Miraculously, I was experiencing the pleasure of witnessing the relief of forgiveness being experienced by both the kids and the adults in the room. And I had a hunch there was about to be a lot of hugs handed out as they went back to their seats. A forgiving God with skin on...their parents.

As far as the east is from the west, so far has He removed our wrong-doings from us. (Psalm 103:12)

For I do not understand what I am doing; for I am not practicing what I want to do, but I do the very thing I hate. (Romans 7:15)

Chapter
FORTY-FOUR
LET THE TREES SING

A favorite family retreat is a little cove called Taylor Bay at the end of a tiny peninsula on Puget Sound. We have also taken our church family there on various occasions, and one Sunday while the choir was there on retreat, we had our Sunday morning worship down on the beach.

When it came time for the children's message, I asked everyone to look over my shoulder at the shoreline where the coming and going of countless tides had eroded away a bank. One of the tall fir trees for which the Northwest is so famous had fallen over. Part of its roots now lay exposed on the bank, and its top pointed seaward. Its original glory was destroyed, and it was now precariously close to becoming driftwood.

Apparently, it had been that way for some time because it had taken some unique action—which I wanted the group to consider.

"Look at the branches still growing on the fallen tree," I pointed out. "If a picture is worth a thousand words, I think you will agree that they each have quite a story to tell." For the next few minutes, I became the tree's storyteller.

"Suddenly finding itself on an even footing with all the other branches after the collapse, the treetop was disoriented, but tried gamely to press on in the same direction it had been pursuing for years.

"Near the tip of the tree you will notice a limb that, at one time, hung gracefully downward from the very top of the tree's foliage. It was quite proud of its place in the scheme of things, being second in command as it were, at the very top of a flourishing organism. Neither it, nor the treetop offshoot, noticed that the foundation of its evergreen empire was eroding dangerously. This happens when you get too far away from your life-giving roots.

"The second-in-command was quick to renew its allegiance to the leader and even shifted its weight so that it too began to grow horizontally. After some time of following the leader in the wrong direction, it suddenly noticed that its tip was very close to being even with the original treetop. It became gripped by a new inspiration that, with a little more effort, it could overtake the original treetop and become the leader itself.

"The next bough in line actually found itself facing the lapping waves. Daily, salt water punished some of its sweeping foliage until a good portion of it fell into the surf and was carried away. The damaged stub that remained, stubbornly climbed out from under

the leaning tree until it finally rose above the trunk with a new zest for living. It looked at the two branches racing toward the horizon and thought, *If I throw my weight with them I could jeopardize us all. The sting of the saltwater is not something I relish experiencing again. Instead, I will grow toward the safety of my Creator.*

"The bough that had originally been just below it had already begun its struggle to follow the treetop. Suddenly, it found itself blocked by the branch that had emerged from under the trunk.

'No,' the little interceptor pleaded, 'Think of what you are doing. If you go that direction, it is certain death to all of us. If you want to live, you must reach for the Creator of life.' The bough wavered somewhat and, occasionally, it was swayed by the two branches it had been following its whole life. Each time it hesitated, the stunted little limb would lean against it, encouraging it to creep skyward.

"Meanwhile, the lowest bough on the tree had been in daily communication with the roots that held the tree to the earthen bank. The root system was confident that it could hold its ground, but the battle for power going on at the other end of the tree was making its efforts all the harder. What it needed to turn the disaster around was a strong point man that would let itself be nourished by the roots and would rise steadfastly in the right direction—heavenward. If it would cultivate limbs of its own, the Creator would bless its fruitfulness.

"As you can see," I told the group, "it is well on its way, even now, to becoming a mature fir tree in its own right. It counterbalances the weight of wrong that could pull them all down."

I let the group consider our object lesson for a while longer, noting the piles of driftwood that spoke of dead tree civilizations from days long gone that had suffered the consequences of growing in the wrong direction.

The children had been attentive to my story but were now anxious to be off exploring the beach. I let them wander away as I concluded my allegory to the remaining adults.

"The Book warns us that false teachers will try to lead us away from following the Way that leads to life. When we follow them, not only do we assure our own destruction but that of those whose lives we touch. The very weight of our opinion can be deadly to someone who has a fragile grasp on which way is right. On the other hand, when a struggling person has a strong believer to lean on, they can be gently guided away from that way that seems right to man, and toward the direction that truly saves.

"The one who can turn the tide for the whole civilization has a firm foundation in the root and finds its strength in the Creator it praises daily. As it grows, it inspires those who are weak and those who have suffered great adversity to find true life. The more these champions rely on each other for encouragement and support, the stronger their influence becomes, and the weaker the followers of the false guides become.

"You will notice that the children have now become part of the story," I gestured toward our rambunctious brood scampering down the beach.

"I aim to capture this scene in my memory, because **our children are the trees of tomorrow.** These little saplings will be studying us, the trees of today, to see which way we will choose for ourselves, and for them."

Lest the memory fade, one of my listeners raised a camera just then; its shutter preserving the moment with a snap.

But false prophets also appeared among the people, just as there will also be false teachers among you, who will secretly introduce destructive heresies, even denying the Master who bought them, bringing swift destruction upon themselves. (2 Peter 2:1)

Then the trees of the forest will sing for joy in the presence of the Lord; *for He is coming to judge the earth.* (1 Chronicles 16:33)

Chapter
FORTY-FIVE
PLAYING TO THE LIGHT

M y husband Bill is blessed with an extremely powerful dramatic tenor voice, but as a choral teacher at a Bible college, he had pretty much stopped using his own voice to teach others how to use theirs. However, you can imagine just how *outside the box* it was when he decided to leave full-time ministry and venture out on the road as a secular entertainer in the 1970s.

We never strayed outside The Book, however, and God used that decade to teach us lessons we could not have gotten in Bible college. Twenty years later when churches struggled with understanding the language of the culture they were trying to reach, we could help them, AND DID!

Together with a drummer and a guitar player, we set out on the road in an old Ford laundry van that would go 50 MPH tops. The owner's manual for our used sound equipment was in German so not very helpful. Our 'roadie' was a dog named after Thelonius Monk, and our cat, JazzPurr perched on Bill's shoulder as he drove. We wore bell-bottoms, platform shoes, sequins and fringes.

The live disco sound of the 70s was like all the cultures in America suddenly came together to create a distinct sound that was both candid and complicated. We covered hundreds of hits and hit makers during that decade with radio disc jockey Wolfman Jack leading the way!

My hubby played bass and sang his heart out! "Proud Mary," "Joy to the World," "Louie Louie," "On the Road Again," and, of course, anything by the Eagles or Elvis, Ozzy or the Osmonds brought the crowded dance floor alive. But when he turned on his power voice for show tunes and ballads such as *Summertime* or *Solitaire*, even those who made their way to the floor for a slow dance, stopped with mouths agape to listen to him.

I have always had a love for music and can play a smattering of instruments. I learned to bang out a rhythm on my tambourine, and without effort, I picked out a harmony part to sing. However, my real flair seemed to be making people happy. On our breaks, I would circulate through the crowded tables and get to know the patrons. Later, as they danced by the stage, I would laugh and joke with them. They would banter with me from their tables, and, just when I thought we had a good thing going, they would ask why I never got to sing something. Aack! I never felt comfortable as a vocal soloist.

I managed to avoid it about ninety percent of the time but, sometimes, I just had to sing a solo. We developed a short repertoire of songs that were covers of radio hits of the era, mostly easy country rock that I could twang out if I had to: "Delta Dawn," "Help Me Make It Through the Night," "Snowbird," *et al.*

I would perform, reluctantly, if a request came in, but I never got over the stage fright that it generated. Suddenly, those friends I had made became a sea of eyes, all glued on me. What if they didn't like me? What if I messed up the words? What if I sang off-key? *What if...?* Then the music intro would start and, like it or not, I was on.

If you have ever been on stage, you will know what a Klieg light is. It uses a tungsten-halogen filament and is roughly equivalent to 10,000 watts. It heralded the era of blinding performers. In the popular musical *Mamma Mia*, ABBA's lyrics, "Super trouper beams are gonna blind me..." describes what we endured for five hours each night.

When I was "in my groove" as a comical source of amusement to the crowd, the light was an extreme annoyance. I would have to squint and, occasionally, even shield my eyes with my hand to see who was talking to me from the candle-lit darkness.

When I had to sing a solo, however, that blinding spotlight instantly became my friend. I would play to the light, singing as if the crowd did not exist. If I messed up, only the light would know.

The light was all that mattered. That was an important takeaway from my time on stage.

As children, talking about Jesus is simple. But as we grow older, we seem to develop tongue-tying inhibitions. Kids seem to have no trouble whatsoever sharing their faith with anyone who will listen. Let's say a school friend admits he is scared of a bully who keeps dissing him and pushing him around. Suddenly, the story of a shepherd boy named David who killed a giant with a slingshot just flows into their conversation "for reals."

When kids talk about God's saving grace through Jesus Christ, they aren't fumbling for the right words to say to convey a theological concept. They are simply telling a friend about another Friend they have who is always there when they need Him, "for reals!"

I have stopped counting how many times I have been told "I can live my faith, but I just can't say the words." Some people even say, "It's not my gift, as if to imply that it is God's fault they can't speak up!"

So, here is a solution. The Book says that Jesus is the Light of the World. If you get the jitters talking about your Savior, try concentrating on the Light of the World. Let His blinding presence block out whatever negative reactions you are anticipating from your friends. They may not like what you have to say, and they may not agree with it, but they will have to admit that your face was, literally, shining with a light they could not explain.

So, when the intro is giving you your cue, don't freeze, don't panic. Just open your mouth, take a deep breath, and play to the Light.

Then Jesus again spoke to them, saying, "I am the Light of the world; the one who follows Me will not walk in the darkness, but will have the Light of life." (John 8:12)

The redeemed of the LORD shall say so... (Psalm 107:2)

He put a new song in my mouth, a song of praise to our God; many will see and fear and will trust in the LORD. (Psalm 40:3)

Chapter
FORTY-SIX

THE
REAL THING

It is a tradition in our home to have a Christmas tree that goes clear to the vaulted ceiling. So, when I found a beautiful 12-foot, artificial, alpine fir Nordstrom display-window tree at a local thrift store, I could not believe my luck!!!

Just think of the advantages! I could store it with the lights still on it and save, not only money, but time.

From the moment I unloaded it out of the back of my car, my oldest daughter Wendie had misgivings.

"You got a fake tree? What were you thinking?"

I assured her it would be beautiful, and we could set evergreen scented candles around the house to make up for the loss of aroma.

"Great," she said, "fake evergreen scent to go with the fake tree!"

Still, I nervously awaited the family's response. My son arrived from the airport, and his first words as he carried his luggage through the room were, "Nice tree, Mom! Good job!"

I looked at my oldest daughter with a smirk as she rolled her eyes and shook her head.

Christmas Eve, we gathered around the lighted tree after church. On Christmas morning, the presents piled around the tree were distributed, and the feasting and merriment began. Friends visited over the next few days, and the tree seemed to be the success that I had hoped it would be.

Finally, about three days later, my son sat down on the couch by the tree and reached through the foliage to plug his laptop computer into the power bar under its limbs.

"Wait a minute," he said indignantly, "that's NOT a real tree!"

"Yes," I agreed, triumphantly, "but it took you three days to discover that, so don't give me any guff."

Except for the slight inconvenience of trying to figure out where to store a 12-foot Christmas tree, I was so delighted at the results of my experiment that I decided to try it again in the Spring when it came time to put out my hanging baskets of geraniums.

Why should I spend all that money on genuine geraniums, when the silk ones from the craft store looked so real? Plus, no more reaching up over my head with the sprinkler and having cold water dribble to places better left un-dribbled. That cinched it! My maintenance-free hanging baskets soon swung lazily from their hooks all around the house.

The next morning, I took my coffee to the porch to bask in the rising sun and enjoy my beautiful new creations. When a hummingbird stopped at the first basket. I chuckled. Wow! They look

so real they even fooled a bird! He stuck his beak into the nearest blossom and then studied it curiously when it yielded nothing sweet. He went on to the next basket with puzzled obstinance.

Finally, he flew past me to the basket on the corner of the house where he appeared to lose patience with the situation. He flew right over to my chair and, at a distance of less than two feet, gave me an exasperated chewing out. After venting his disapproval, the bird flew away.

Properly chastened, I reviewed what I had done from a different perspective. Was I going to say the same thing I said to my son about the fake tree?

"No, it is not real, but even you were fooled by it at first, so don't give me any guff!"

Somehow, it didn't have the same effect.

The next morning when the hummingbird visited, he stuck his beak into the first basket to see if anything had changed. Nope! He flew away, and I never saw him again. The plant was not what it presented itself to be. It wasn't real, and he hurried off to find something that was. My second-rate shortcut cost me a friend.

It made me think about the fake things in my life. What, in my Christian walk, misrepresents Christ to my friends? Things like gossiping, chuckling at jokes God would not approve of, and not making it right when a clerk gives me back too much change, may seem harmlessly dishonest. However, after a while, friends who are wanting to know what a real Christian is are saying, "Honestly, I'm not seeing a lot of difference between your lifestyle and mine."

Sadly, the world we live in sometimes encourages us to "fake it 'til you make it." The Book, on the other hand, tells us to "be transformed." That means being *really* changed from the inside out. It doesn't mean substitute the 'old nature' with a 'fake Christianity' that will, sooner or later, give itself away. If it only takes a hummingbird a quick dip into a silk flower to know it is fake, you can be very sure that people are going to be just as quick to see a phony Christian when they spot one.

When you don't follow The Book, when you aren't real as a follower of Christ, when you behave as one who has not allowed Christ to transform, what are you going to say?

"Yes, I am a hypocrite, but I fooled you for a while, so don't give me any guff!"

I don't think so! Not only will you lose an opportunity to share something *real* with someone searching for *reality*, but your deception will cause very real damage. Your friend will be much more cautious in the future about what and who they believe.

We absorb a daily diet of "pseudo" and "virtual" and "cyber." Marketing slogans use words like "faux" instead of "phony" and "pleather" instead of plastic leather to convince us that something fake is as good as the real thing.

The plaster and paint imitations of ice cream cakes in a display case might look mouthwatering but, I guarantee, they would leave a really bad taste in your mouth.

Just so, always being "sincere" and "authentic" and "genuine" has a delicious perk: you will never disappoint or offend or hurt someone who is expecting the REAL thing.

And do not be conformed to this world, but be transformed by the renewing of your mind, so that you may prove what the will of God is, that which is good and acceptable and perfect. (Romans 12:2)

Chapter
FORTY-SEVEN
KNOWING
IMPORTANT
STUFF

At one time, Luke was the smallest member of our congregation. When he had just gotten his stubby legs under him, he was prone to wander among the pews during the service. He laid his head in welcoming laps and stretched out his chubby arms to be picked up by just about anyone. He had a sober little face with big blue eyes and was absolutely irresistible to one and all.

At the end of the service one morning, when the acolyte had just reached the altar with her long brass candlelighter to extinguish the candles, she heard the sound of little feet running up the center aisle. She turned to see Luke crawling up the steps toward her. Instead of continuing, she stopped, reached down, and scooped him up. Together they approached the altar where she helped him extend the wick to the flame until it caught. Then she turned it, so the snuffer covered the first candle and helped him hold it until all of the candles were extinguished. With a look of serene solemnity, Luke continued to grasp the lighted "commission" flame, as the acolyte carried both, him and it, out of the sanctuary.

It was one of those moments you wanted to suspend in time, because our adorable cherubs seem to grow up overnight. Sure enough, in the twinkling of an eye, Luke was celebrating his second birthday. Life in the fast lane went racing on.

Several "Twelfth Man" T-shirts were spotted among the parishioners as they took their seats in church on a crisp fall Sunday, well into football season. It was a pointed reminder to the worship team and the pastor that a big game was scheduled that afternoon; the service should not "go into overtime."

When it came time for the children's message, I said to the congregation, "In the interest of certain time constraints this morning, I will have the children remain with their parents. That ought to carve at least a minute or two off the service." They all nodded, approvingly.

"I am going to play a game this morning, and I choose as my contestant...Luke." As he toddled toward me, I admonished the children and adults to be very quiet and not to give away answers to the questions I was about to ask him. He was already about halfway up my leg when I hoisted him to my hip.

"Luke, can I ask you some questions this morning?" He nodded, gravely. "OK, here we go. Who are the quarterbacks for today's football game?" He opened his mouth like he was about to reply but then shyly dropped his head when he realized he didn't know the answer. I hugged him and assured him it was no big deal. "Let's try another one. What are the stats for the football teams contending for the playoffs?"

This brought a round of noise from the room—chuckles, snorts, and one under-the-breath mutter that "I wasn't being fair, a two-year old can't understand a word like 'stat.' " I shushed them all as Luke buried his head in my shoulder, visibly embarrassed.

"You just pay them no attention. They are only jealous because I picked you to play the game. Are you ready for another question?"

He looked around the congregation, not sure if he wanted to continue or not. Everybody smiled at him. His mom blew him a kiss. Finally, he nodded, reluctantly. "OK, then, last question:"

"Where does Jesus live?"

This time there was no hesitation, not even a hint of doubt. He pointed to his chest and said clearly, "In mine heart."

You could have heard a pin drop as I looked around the room, making eye contact with as many as I could. Then, when Luke realized that he had lost my full attention, he took my cheek in his palm and tapped my chest with his other hand, "In your heart," he said, sincerely. In that instant, I saw an awful lot of teary eyes. In fact, I had to wait a second for the lump in my throat to go away before I could speak.

"Luke, how old are you?" He held two fingers up as straight as he could.

"Only two? Wow, just two years old and you already know the answer to the most important question anyone will ever ask you. Ladies and sports fans, we have a winner," and I handed him a little trophy with a grin. The entire congregation was applauding and cheering as I lowered him to the floor.

Returning to sit with the congregation, I could tell from the way several sports enthusiasts seemed sheepishly preoccupied with the back of the seats in front of them that they were more than willing to concede the match.

I also had the distinct impression that the answers to the first two questions had, for the time being, vanished into the recesses of every mind in the room, replaced by a tiny child with truly important stuff.

Truly I say to you, unless you change and become like children, you will not enter the kingdom of heaven. (Matthew 18:3)

THE "HEAVENLY HOST" WITH SARAH, THE STABLE-CHOMPING DONKEY

Chapter
FORTY-EIGHT
AT THE RIGHT TIME

While no one bats an eye at driving in the rain in the Pacific Northwest, a single snowflake is enough to put the region into a tizzy. Occasionally, when a significant amount of snow has blanketed the region, a telephone tree will announce that church has been canceled due to weather. But, if the pastor and the worship team are able to make it, they turn the heat on and get ready to worship with whomever shows up.

It was just such a day that I set out in adverse conditions to cover the five miles between home and church to deliver my customary children's message for the day.

At the time church was due to start, I was only halfway there. I called the pastor on his cell phone. He answered with,

"Oops, I forgot to turn my phone off. Church has started. Are you OK?"

"Yes," I answered, "It is slow going but I will be there in time for the children's message. Did everybody make it?"

"Not yet," and he mentioned a couple of people who said they were coming but were not there yet.

"Maybe you ought to leave your phone on just in case I need to reach you, or somebody else in the congregation gets into trouble on the road," I suggested.

"Good idea," he agreed, "be safe. Bye"

As soon as I hung up, I called one of the others still on the way.

"Hi, are you still on the road?" I asked.

"Yes, there is a car blocking the lane, but I can't turn around either, so I guess we are stuck here until something moves," was the reply.

"Well, I just talked to the pastor," I said, "and I think it would be a good idea if you called him to let him know so they don't worry. While you're at it, could you tell him that I still plan to get there in time for the children's message?"

"Will do, see you soon," and we signed off.

After a few more minutes of slipping and sliding, I finished the second part of the journey. My phone rang for another round of phone tag. It was the pastor.

"Are you still coming?" he asked.

"Yes, I am on the home stretch, just another mile. I'll be there."

"Well, if you don't make it in time, we can just skip the children's message and move on."

"No, I'll be there but thanks for the offer," I replied.

As I waited at the stoplight, just before the church driveway, I called him one last time.

"OK, I am just about to turn into the parking lot. When it's time for the children's message, have the kids get ready for it. I'll be there," and I hung up so I could concentrate on the slippery parking lot.

It was still a treacherous slide to the church doorway, but I opened it just as he finished settling the kids in their circle around him.

"I'm here!" I announced from the doorway.

"Yay!" the kids chorused.

The extroverted young spokesman for the bunch said,

"We couldn't figure out why we were getting in our circle when you weren't even here."

"Didn't you get my messages that I was coming?" I asked.

"Yeah, you should have seen the pastor's face every time the phone rang during church," they giggled. "Then you still weren't here, and we saw him make a phone call. When it started ringing again, he said, 'Oh no, something must have happened to her.' But this time when he hung up, he told us to come on up and get in our circle."

As they all chimed in to relay the chain of events, I shook my head.

"No, actually, I was just calling to tell him to be ready because I would get here right on time," I chided, "and here I am, right on time!" The congregation broke into applause.

"You know, The Book tells us that when sin came into the world it brought death with it. That is WHY God planned to send His Son *at just the right time* to save us from the sentence of death that is the result of sin.

He sent prophets to remind us, repeatedly, that the Savior was coming. In The Book we read how they told us about his family tree; WHAT tribe he would be born into, and that he would be one of King David's descendants. They said WHERE he would be born, and the prophet Daniel even said WHEN he would be born.

"Each year our church performs the Christmas story of how Joseph, and Mary, who was expecting Jesus, had to make a long dangerous trip to Bethlehem, just when Jesus was about to be born." The kids smiled, remembering their own roles in the Living Nativity.

"My five miles in the snow in my car was nothing compared to what they went through traveling to Bethlehem." My audience went quiet as they nodded in comprehension. "At least," I quipped, "I didn't have to ride a donkey."

The former "stablehand" who had been in charge of Sarah, our live Christmas pageant donkey, did an eye roll and grumbled,

"Sarah kept chewing on the side of the stable and I couldn't get her to stop."

"Yes," I agreed, "donkeys can be very stubborn, so I can't imagine what Joseph had to go through to keep his donkey moving when it got tired.

"The point is, however, that God picked out the perfect time for Jesus to arrive and kept in close communication with His people to assure them that He had not forgotten His promise.

"The Book tells us that '*In the fullness of time, God sent His Son.*' Despite the hardship, despite the waiting, despite the skepticism, despite the human tendency to have a back-up plan, just in case God doesn't come through, Jesus came, just as God said He would. He was right on time."

For the wages of sin is death, but the gracious gift of God is eternal life in Christ Jesus our Lord. (Romans 6:23)

But when the fullness of the time came, God sent His Son, born of a woman, born under the Law. (Galatians 4:4)

Chapter
FORTY-NINE

WHATEVER

"My office thought it would be fun to have a Halloween costume contest at work. I went to the party dressed as Santa Claus." The kids gathered around me rolled their eyes and smacked their foreheads.

"Hey, you're a little early," my boss, Steve, said.

"To which I replied, 'Have you looked in the stores lately?' "

"He thought about it for a minute and then asked, 'Could I borrow your costume tonight?' " I grinned at the kids and rolled my eyes back at them!

"What is it you kids all say, when something happens that you don't even think is worth responding to? I put my finger to my lips and began thinking out loud, "Like...like..."

Finally, Sarah, one of the older girls ventured with a dramatic flare, "Like, Whatever!"

"That's it! I hear kids say it all the time." I struck a Valley Girl pose and said, "Well, when I walk into a store in September and see Halloween goods on one side of the aisle and Christmas goods on the other side, I just want to go, 'Like, whatevah!'

"So when I made a family rule that Christmas shopping had to be done by Labor Day weekend (not kidding), or you had to MAKE the present, you can guess what my kids said, right?"

"Like, Whatevah!" The group was so vehement when they yelled it, I had the distinct impression they didn't think much of my rule either.

"Yeah, it took some time for it catch on but when I refused to take them Christmas shopping in December, I got some pretty incredible hand-made gifts. By the time they could drive themselves, they were already shopping the sales year round and loving it. They would hear someone say, 'Boy, I wish I had...' and they would file that inside information away in their shopping list.

"The best part was not being out there with all those people who were frantically racing around at the last minute to get gifts."

At this I took a deep breath and plunged ahead. "...for their *family* and *friends* and *bosses* and *co-workers* and *mailman* and *paper carrier* and just *a couple extra* in case they forgot someone."

I panted and signaled the kids to hold on a sec while I caught my breath and then went on. "Instead, the real Christmas season in our home could be devoted to the GIFT OF GOD, His Son, our Savior.

"When the school system realized that not all of the new cultures that were coming to America celebrated Christmas, it decided to change what used to be called 'Christmas Break' to 'Winter Break.' When I saw this sign go up as the year-end break began, I had to applaud the custodian's solution.

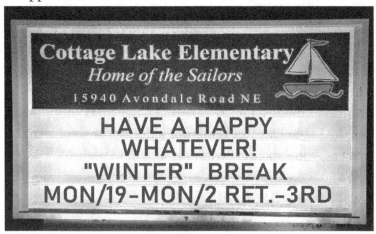

"I thought about the apostle Paul when he was at Mars Hill in Greece. He noticed an inscription on an altar that read 'to an unknown God.' Those people were doing the very same thing today's Christmas shoppers are doing when they buy an extra gift just to be on the safe side in case they forgot someone. So, you know what Paul did?"

The kids all shook their heads, collectively.

"He took that opportunity to tell them about the one true God, the God they didn't know. Their worldly standards didn't change Paul's godly standards, and they shouldn't change ours.

"Many times, The Book defines our role as being *in the world but not of the world*. So...WHAT-EVER!"

That brought on another thunderous round of WHATEVAH in agreement.

"But wait—it gets better," I hinted as I unzipped the vest over my new sweatshirt.

The kids quieted down and leaned in.

"What are the odds that I would stumble on this item on sale in the AMEN Christian Bookstore? I am sure the Holy Spirit led me to that rack of hoodies on purpose.

"There it was, in black and white, the PERFECT solution to the dilemma about what to celebrate in December. The school custodian, unwittingly, had it correct! We SHOULD celebrate WHAT-EVER, not just in December, but every day!

Together, the kids read the verse from The Book that was printed on my shirt.

"If we would give our attention and our devotion to all those things that are true, noble, right, pure, lovely, admirable, excellent, or praise-worthy, our God would be glorified. If we would act on those things in the name of the Christ, for whom Christmas is named, who knows WHATEVER might be the fruits of our actions in the years to come?"

So Paul...said, "Men of Athens, I see that you are very religious in all respects. For while I was passing through and examining the objects of your worship, I also found an altar with this inscription, 'TO AN UNKNOWN GOD.' Therefore, what you worship in ignorance, this I proclaim to you. The God who made the world and everything that is in it, since He is Lord of heaven and earth, does not dwell in temples made by hands; nor is He served by human hands, as though He needed anything, since He Himself gives to all people life and breath and all things; and He made from one man every nation of mankind to live on all the face of the earth, having determined their appointed times and the boundaries of their habitation, that they would seek God, if perhaps they might feel around for Him and find Him, though He is not far from each one of us; for in Him we live and move and exist... (Acts 17:22-34)

They are not of the world, just as I am not of the world. (John 17:16)

...whatever is true, whatever is honorable, whatever is right, whatever is pure, whatever is lovely, whatever is commendable, if there is any excellence and if anything worthy of praise, think about these things. (Philippians 4:8)

Chapter
FIFTY
EVERYBODY NEEDS A HIPPO

"One summer day, my mischievous teenage daughter Brie told me she had gotten my birthday present but couldn't wait until fall to give it. What could I do?

"You won't believe what was inside." The kids all leaned in wondering what birthday present could be so special. "In the box was the head of a hippo joined by a hose to a tiny pump."

The puzzled faces of my audience meant I needed a graphic and so I showed the church gang gathered in front of me a picture of my hippo head spurting water from its nostrils as if the rest of its body was submerged in my pond.

"Now if someone asked me, Hey, do you want a hippo for a birthday present?' I would have said, 'NO!' and even if they said, 'you need a hippo in your pond,' I would have argued, 'I don't think so. Hippos are very large, and my pond is very small.'

"However, now that I have my hippo head, I cannot imagine my pond without it! My hippo is the first thing I see in the morning when I open the bedroom curtains and the last thing I see before I close them at night. It makes me laugh both times.

"Ahhhh!" I said, suddenly, snapping my fingers. "That reminds me! I just thought of a great song to get stuck in your head. It's about a little girl who wanted a hippopotamus!" I got no further as they all interrupted, blurting out,

"FOR CHRISTMAS!"

"Yep," I grinned, "and *only* a hippopotamus would do! Gayla Peevey was only ten years old when she recorded, "I Want a Hippopotamus for Christmas," and, to no one's great surprise, it stayed high on the Billboard charts for many weeks.

"She sings of her great joy and surprise on Christmas morning when she creeps down the stairs, opens her eyes, and sees a hippo standing under the tree.

"All I could think was that her Christmas tree living room must be a whole lot bigger than mine. If a hippo could get through my front door, it would be as big as my living room and there would be nothing left but one squashed Christmas tree!"

The kids all giggled in agreement, and a couple of the moms added their emphatic disapproval.

"Do you know that the little girl singer actually DID get a hippo for Christmas?! A fund-raising campaign brought in enough donations to purchase a hippo named Matilda that was presented to her—you guessed it—on Christmas morning.

"Of course, it was too big for her house, so Matilda was donated to the zoo, where she lived fifty years and millions of people got to enjoy her!

"You all seem to know that song, but did you know it was first recorded in 1953? Then it was re-released sixty years later, and it went viral AGAIN. The more people who listen to a song on the radio,

the higher the rating goes on the charts, and the longer the stations keep playing it. The more the hippo song is heard, the more
a hippopotamus shows up on Christmas wish lists. Stores know to
keep tabs on what is viral and stock their shelves with puny repli-
cas of the real thing to satisfy the demands."

After a brief pause, I resumed talking, dropping my voice, conspiratorially.

"Do you know that there is a gift given to us at Christmas that is
even bigger than a hippo?" The kids looked at me wide-eyed and
some shook their heads.

"The HUGE gift of forgiveness brought by the tiny baby in the
manger is much huger and amazing than finding a hippo beneath
your tree. Because, long after the other presents we found under
the tree have been broken or outgrown, the gift of forgiveness will
still be important to us.

"If something about Jesus hit the charts like Gayla's hippo, how
high do you think its ratings would go?

The kids shrugged, collectively, but I had a 'gotcha' ready. In my
best kid voice I shouted, desperately, "Isn't there anyone out there
who can tell me what Christmas is all about?"

"Charlie Brown!" The whole room announced, unanimously.

"Yep, just a few years later, *A Charlie Brown Christmas* was first
aired on TV. I get the impression you have all seen it." Hands went
up and parents nodded.

"You see, that has become a true Christmas classic. Linus says,
'Sure, Charlie Brown,' and then proceeds to tell the whole world
the Christmas story straight out of The Book. In 1965, it went just
as VIRAL as the Christmas Hippo had earlier. It has received more
awards and remained a family favorite for the ages for over fifty
years! We need to continue telling the story like Linus told Charlie
Brown in the TV special."

Everyone clapped appreciatively, including the pastor.

"How many of you have a nativity display with the baby Jesus in a manger among your Christmas decorations?"

All hands waved excitedly.

"What if suddenly, a bright heavenly light came right through your roof and lit up the whole room?"

I looked up toward the ceiling and then shielded my squinted eyes with my forearms. The kids' eyes all followed my gaze.

"Then, what if you saw a host of angels fill the sky?" My left arm made a huge arc from the front to the back of the room. Their heads followed the arc and then continued to swivel in unison when my right arm made a wide arc from one side of the room to the other.

"Then, when it looked like the sky could not hold even one more, you heard the whole army of them begin praising God for His good news of great joy for all people, just as they did the night our Savior, the great GIFT from God was born? Christmas as we know it would never be the same." Then I whispered, "I don't think I would ever be the same either.

"No, everybody does NOT need a hippo. What they NEED is a reality check about what Christmas is all about; the HUGE gift of God that saves us for eternity with Him. It is up to us to make it go VIRAL!"

For God so loved the world, that He gave His only Son, so that everyone who believes in Him will not perish, but have eternal life. (John 3:16)

For by grace you have been saved through faith; and this is not of yourselves, it is the gift of God. (Ephesians 2:8)

And an angel of the Lord suddenly stood near them, and the glory of the Lord shone around them; and they were terribly frightened. And so the angel said to them, "Do not be afraid; for behold, I bring you good news of great joy which will be for all the people. (Luke 2:9-10)

And suddenly there appeared with the angel a multitude of the heavenly army of angels praising God and saying, "Glory to God in the highest, and on earth peace among people with whom He is pleased." (Luke 2:13–14)

THE FRIENDLY BEASTS TOLD SANDIE AND THE LITTLEST ANGEL THEIR VERSION OF THE NATIVITY STORY, THEN ALL PILED INTO AND ON THE ROCKING LOVESEAT WITH BABY JESUS AND SANG THIS CZECH LULLABY:

Little Jesus, sweetly sleep, do not stir. We will lend a coat of fur.
We will rock you, rock you, rock you. We will rock you, rock you, rock you.
See the fur to keep you warm. Snugly round your tiny form

THE ROCKER WAS NEVER QUITE RIGHT AFTER THAT BUT THE PAGEANT WAS A HIT!

CHRISTMAS BONUS:
NO ROOM AT THE INN

My daughter Wendie and I headed for our adventure of a lifetime in the Highlands of Scotland. Because we planned to meander as we wished, stay longer in one place if we wanted, and take various detours if we had the urge, we made no advance reservations.

Heading from Edinburgh to Inverness, we noted that our bus was packed. Though we had plenty of time to phone for accommodations on the long ride, we learned the hostels were full, as were the B & Bs. There was a major hotel, but we were on a tight budget, so we didn't even consider it. By the time the bus pulled into the station, we still had nowhere to sleep for the night.

I was beginning to feel like Mary must have felt when she and Joseph arrived in Bethlehem where, instead of a comfy room and a hot meal, she was welcomed with the unmistakable first pangs of labor. My bad knee had cramped up on the long bus trip, and it was killing me. I could barely walk and, had there been one available, like Mary, I would gladly have straddled a donkey.

We gamely made the rounds of the lodging sites Wendie had called just to make sure there hadn't been any cancellations. Finally, in desperation we trekked to the grand hotel with its beckoning bright lights and its polished concierge desk. Gulp!

The Scottish lass seemed surprised to see us standing at her counter.

"Canna help ye?" she asked.

"We've come a long way today and need a room for the night."

"Did ye have reservations?" She asked a little nervously, "We are already full, and I wasna expectin' anyone else."

"No," we admitted, "we had no idea things would be so crowded in Inverness."

"Well, usually they are na, but this is a three-day holiday weekend, so families and college students from the lowlands are takin' a wee vacation."

That explained the crowded buses and lodging. I sized up the comfortable looking chairs in the lobby.

"Is your restaurant still open?" I asked, resignedly.

"Aye, right through those doors over there. Ye can leave your luggage with me if ye like." She, obviously, wanted to be helpful.

We ordered sparingly, but even an appetizer of haggis, neeps, and tatties did not come cheap. The waiter cleared our plates, but we stayed as long as we could until we were the only dining patrons left and the staff wanted to close up. As we stood to leave, my aching knee reminded me I wouldn't be getting rest that evening and opted for a couch in the lobby to stretch my leg.

Wendie headed for the tourist pamphlet rack to find us reservations for the next night. As I waited for her, I couldn't help but think about that miraculous Nativity so long ago, when it seemed the whole world had descended upon Bethlehem. Mary and Joseph could find no room at the inn. Like our predicament, all the rooms were taken for the night, but, while I might have to nurse my hurting knee in the lobby all night, I sure wouldn't want to deliver a baby there.

My daughter had spent so much time trying to find lodging, that I felt badly and wondered if our adventure had been more of a misadventure. I prayed, fervently, that our Father in heaven would guide her efforts.

Poor Joseph. How helpless he must have felt as he watched Mary's labor pains intensify as the hours dragged on. It must have been absolute desperation that led him to approach the innkeeper again to ask for anything, any space at all, that would give his weary wife a little relief.

"Your stable?" I could just hear him saying. "Yes, yes, the stable would be just fine. I'm sure our donkey won't mind sharing his stall with us." With relief he could tell his expectant wife, "Mary, you are not going to believe this. They found room for us after all."

I was still lost in these musings when my daughter returned with good news that she had found a room for the next night. We laughed with relief, both thinking it would be presumptuous to expect God to also answer our prayer for this night.

"Well, it wouldn't hurt to ask again, I suppose, and I need to get my toothbrush out of my luggage anyway," I said as I struggled to my feet. Wendie helped me limp across to the counter where we asked if by some miracle, a room had been found.

"Well, if ye dinna mind sharing a wee room, one of our guests has had to depart suddenly. He will be checking out shortly."

"We'll take it!" We said in unison.

"Ye can register now if ye like." she said as she quoted us an amount that was half of what we were expecting, "But ye'll have to wait until we can clean it before it is ready."

I started to chuckle as I thought of Mary and Joseph being so relieved that they could sleep in the stable and then she and my daughter must have thought I had lost my mind when I said,

"Oh, just throw down a little fresh straw and we'll be good to go!"

And she gave birth to her firstborn son; and she wrapped Him in cloths, and laid Him in a manger, because there was no room for them in the inn. (Luke 2:7)

Chapter
FIFTY-ONE
CARRY
THE
LIGHT

"**I** was cleaning one day and, as I reached over the upright back of an antique pump organ with the vacuum cleaner wand, I felt something suck up against the crevice tool. Too late, I remembered what was there. Two candlesticks - unique because they had stems but no bases. Not able to stand them up anywhere, I had laid them in what I thought was a safe place. Climbing up on the organ bench, I picked up all the pieces of the broken one and dropped them in a baggy then lowered myself carefully to the floor.

"I stood there holding my last candlestick in one hand and the baggy full of broken glass in the other thinking to myself, 'Now what?' Just then I happened to catch sight of an old gospel song-book sitting on the organ. The title of the page open was, 'Carry the Light.'

"Our God has a great sense of humor. I looked at the candlestick in my hand and then back at the gospel song, my mind racing with instant spiritual insight. **Don't put it down!**"

I explained what had happened as I held it in my hand for my curious young crowd to see as they filed up the church aisles toward me.

"The Book tells us to *let our light shine before men*, because if our good deeds bring a little light into their life, they may stop and think. 'Hey, they did that for me because they are a Christ-follower.

Who is this God they serve? I want to know more.'

"I know it may sound a little silly, but I wonder what kind of a reaction I would get if I were carrying my lighted candle around with me everywhere I went.

" 'Whatcha doin?'

" 'What's *that* for?'

" 'How come you're carrying a *candle*?' Not to mention those who don't say a word. They just walk away from the crazy lady, shaking their heads.

"But," I said as I lit a flame in my candleholder, "If I were the *only* light in a very dark room, I would suddenly, be very popular. Then, if I told them that my little light was nothing compared to *Jesus*, the Light of the World, they might stop and think about it. If I were the only flame available on a cold night with which to light a campfire, people would suddenly be coming closer. If, when I lit the fire, I told them that I had a fire inside me that would never go out, they might ask me about it.

"Unfortunately, carrying a candle around with us all the time is not possible. In fact, it is not even legal." I looked up sadly at the congregation. "You kids might not know this, but there are even fire code regulations we have to follow when we light candles in our church."

I held up the little baggy of broken shards for everyone to see. It clinked forlornly as I told them, "On the other hand, the light of the gospel is something that God alone has power over, and He wants us to spread it like fire. It is not something we can put down any more than this candlestick can be put down. It can't be wasted, it can't be extinguished, it can't be saved for later.

"It CAN grow into a mighty blaze that The Book says will bring glory to God if we carry the Light everywhere we go, and never *ever* put it down."

Then Jesus again spoke to them, saying, "I am the Light of the world; the one who follows Me will not walk in the darkness, but will have the Light of life." (John 8:12)

You are the light of the world. A city set on a hill cannot be hidden; nor do people light a lamp and put it under a basket, but on the lampstand, and it gives light to all who are in the house. Your light must shine before people in such a way that they may see your good works, and glorify your Father who is in heaven. (Matthew 5:14-16)

For you were once darkness, but now you are light in the Lord; walk as children of light. (Ephesians 5:8)

For you are all children of light and children of the day. We do not belong to the night or the darkness. (1 Thessalonians 5:5, CSB)

Author SANDIE WILLIAMS during a writing session

Chapter
FIFTY-TWO
YOU WILL REMEMBER THIS

We had become 'empty nesters,' and it seemed that my days of interacting with the church children might be drawing to a close. Not being part of the active worship team was taking some getting used to on my part as I parked myself in a pew with the rest of the parishioners.

One day, the service was closing with a majestic old hymn. I recalled it almost word for word from the more traditional services of my childhood and was singing it, joyfully.

Suddenly, two little girls who were about four years of age, began to disrupt the song. ShayMarie and Kelsey had found some colorful scarves in the children's room and were now racing up and down the center aisle, laughing gleefully, with the colored streamers flowing behind them as they ran.

Perhaps I was taking my unaccustomed "maturity" a little too seriously, but my immediate reaction was, "I wish somebody would snag those two; they are ruining the music for everybody." The thought had no sooner occurred, when a clear, small voice in my head said, "You will remember this. Someday, when the happy sounds of little ones are scarce in My sanctuary, you will remember this." Gulp! Contritely, I closed my eyes to sing the rest of the anthem and, by the time it was done, I was convinced that the accompanying laughter had turned the sacred old song into a spiritual experience of corporate praise ascending to heaven.

That was years ago, and do you know that I cannot remember what the hymn was, but I can still hear the laughter, and I have never forgotten the image of those scarves billowing like cherub wings as those two tiny saints danced before the Lord.

A few years later, another family began visiting that same local church before they relocated out of our area. Fourteen-year-old Sammy suffered from Myelin Atrophy, a birth-related condition that severely stunted his development. His progress was, at that point, about an eighteen-month level. He could not articulate words, but there was absolutely nothing wrong with his vocal cords. When the congregation sang, he bellowed along, and, when the pastor preached, he often offered comments in a language known only to him, speaking in tongues, as it were.

The first day that he was there, I could tell that the row of senior citizens directly in front of him were disturbed by the racket. I have since learned that sharp noises are painfully deafening to those wearing hearing aids. I thought to myself, "OK, huge problem!" The thought had no sooner occurred, when a clear, small voice in my head said, "You will remember this. Someday when the innocent sounds of afflicted ones are scarce in My sanctuary, you will remember this." From then on, when Sammy accompanied his family to church, he had his own reserved seat in the front row where nothing separated him from the altar, his praises ascending, pleasing, and wholly acceptable to his heavenly Father.

Drugs had destroyed Brian's mind and his body, and he was reduced to sleeping outside, his mental faculties hazy and his former lithe military body, flabby and bloated. One day, much like the story of King Nebuchadnezzar in The Book, he lifted his eyes to heaven. Lurching out of the neighborhood park where he camped, he went into an adjacent church and told the pastor, "I need help."

Pastor Ken and his congregation assisted him in getting treatment, and when he began worshiping in the local church where I met him, he was living in a halfway house within walking distance.

I never saw anyone who could worship like Brian. He was filled with an inner glow that lit up the room around him. He loved to sit right next to the worship band, and even as the sanctuary began to fill up, his customary seat would stay empty until he emerged from the room where he attended the adult Bible Study.

One Sunday, when he did not show up for Bible Study, I excused myself from the group to go and get him. I found him in the sanctuary, where he had discovered the room had not been vacuumed after a function the evening before. I quietly froze in my tracks and watched him. Although the hand that guided the wand of the vacuum never stopped as he cleaned his Lord's sanctuary, every few seconds he would look up as if he could actually see Him and say, "Thank you, Jesus." "I love you, Lord." With tears streaming down my face, I returned to the Bible Study without him.

Although I wondered if Brian actually understood what was said to him, I always stopped to chat with him before the service. One day I found myself complaining to him, questioning whether God really heard me when I prayed. He interrupted my babbling with, "Sandie, God always hears everything you pray." He said nothing more, but a clear, small voice in my head said, "You will remember this. Someday when truth spoken by my anointed ones is scarce in My sanctuary, you will remember this."

Until I met Brian's twin sister at his memorial service, I had begun to wonder if he was actually an angel that we were entertaining unaware.

I wrote this chapter with tears dropping on the keyboard, as I mourn the state of our world today, and I ache for the children who may never know any other way unless WE, who remember, pass it on to them. My days of interacting with the little ones did not then and, hopefully, never will draw to a close.

I find myself listening for my granddaughter, Rowan, who should arrive at my door any second now. I try to write when she is not around so I can concentrate better, and her boisterous antics are not distracting me. Right now, however, I seem to need my granddaughter to invade my space with her exuberance. In fact, all of a sudden, I hear a clear, small voice in my head saying, "You will remember this."

Let's not become discouraged in doing good, for in due time we will reap, if we do not become weary. So then, while we have opportunity, let's do good to all people, and especially to those who are of the household of the faith. (Galatians 6:9-10)

Years ago, our church choir was going to perform Handel's Messiah as an event for the community. We pulled out all the stops. The director booked several professional singers to do the solo parts. He procured two keyboard players, one to play organ and the other to provide a full orchestra on synthesizer. Lastly, he retained a light man to operate a spotlight from the rear of the sanctuary.

Finally, the big night came. The spotlight came on, and the keyboardists launched into the rousing introduction of the oratorio as the choir stood poised to sing.

Suddenly, about fifty-two measures into the music, the power went off. The director stood, baton raised and mouth open. The custodian from the congregation who knew about such things, ran to flip the circuit breaker and got the show back on track.

Fifty-two measures into the second attempt, it happened again. This time, several men from the congregation jumped up from their seats. They had just recently been responsible for upgrading the wiring in the kitchen so it could handle multiple electric griddles on separate circuits. Recognizing the symptoms of a similar power overload, they set off to round up an extension cord long enough to reach to the other end of the church where the kitchen was.

While they executed their plan of removing the spotlight from the same circuit that the organ and synthesizer were on, the director recovered his composure and turned to face the audience.

With a chagrined look on his face he said, "I have heard that it took Handel just one week to compose Messiah. It is beginning to look like it will take us a week to perform it."

The listening audience roared with appreciative laughter, and his comment broke the ice. People began conversing with visitors sitting next to them while the problem was being remedied. Thanks to these glitches in man's timing, God's timing was perfected. By the time the performance commenced in earnest, new friendships had begun all over the room. I felt like God looked down and saw that it was good.

I decided that my book was going to be fifty-two chapters long; one for each week of the year. The Book says that Nehemiah finished rebuilding the wall of Jerusalem in just fifty-two days. Well, there you go. I *certainly* ought to be able to write a chapter a day. Yet the manuscript I expected to have done in just fifty-two days, took years to complete!

One chapter a day turned into one chapter a week, turned into one chapter a month. Meanwhile, life is happening at its usual frenetic pace around me, dictating other priorities that I should be attending to along the way. Maybe someday I will write another volume about those things too.

There was always one constant, however. The Holy Spirit never let me down; always steering me toward *outside the box* content relating to stories from *inside The Book* for the kids and I to bring to life each week. The worship leader's screeching sound system feedback in chapter 9 is a prime example. I don't even remember what had been my original topic that day before the Holy Spirit inspired an impromptu change of plan!

I close what I hope has been a refreshing romp for the child in each of us, with the prayer I breathed each time I finished an episode:

Father, may my efforts be to Your Glory. If I have erred in any way in faithfully following Your spiritual direction, please erase it from the minds of all who read this or hear false words. Where I have spoken Truth, I thank you for the Holy Spirit's guidance, and ask that You imprint it indelibly on our hearts for Jesus sake. Amen and AMEN.

So the wall was completed on the twenty-fifth of the month Elul, in fifty-two days. (Nehemiah 6:15)

We also speak these things, not in words taught by human wisdom, but in those taught by the Spirit, combining spiritual thoughts with spiritual words. (1 Corinthians 2:13)

About the Author

SANDIE WILLIAMS has spent a lifetime turning spiritual nuggets found in everyday events into parables and vignettes her readers and listeners can relate to.

She is a seasoned word warrior with degrees in theology and English, drawing on an inexhaustible supply of anecdotal episodes from her mixed bag of careers and travels.

Sandie and her husband Bill share their fifth-generation family homestead in rural Washington state with their children and grandchildren. "It may feel like Casa de Chaos," she says, "but it has spiritual nuggets just waiting to be found!"

Made in the USA
Middletown, DE
20 June 2024